UNCLE JOHN'S ORIGINAL BREAD BOOK

"No nation can be destroyed while it possesses a good home life."

—J. G. HOLLAND

Uncle John's
ORIGINAL BREAD BOOK

Recipes for Breads, Biscuits,
Griddle Cakes, Rolls, Crackers, Etc.

by

John Rahn Braué

Illustrated by Herb McKinley

GALAHAD BOOKS · NEW YORK CITY

Library of Congress Catalog Card Number: 73-91801

ISBN 0-88365-143-2

Published by arrangement with Exposition Press, Inc.

Printed in the United States of America

DESIGNED BY AMJAD N. QURESHI

To

homes everywhere

"*There is no spectacle on earth more appealing than that of a beautiful woman in the act of cooking dinner for someone she loves.*"—THOMAS WOLFE

"*Our Constitution is in actual operation: everything appears to promise that it will last; but in this world nothing is certain but death and taxes.*"—BENJAMIN FRANKLIN

PREFACE

"Forty is the old age of youth: fifty is the youth of old age."
—Hugo

If you are of the vintage years, you will remember with keen nostalgia the aroma of yeast breads baking and the taste sensation of the home-baked treats—hot breads dripping with country butter; tender memories of school lunches of cheese and pumpernickel; crunchy oatmeal cookies and cold milk. Those were the times of open summer streetcars with the impatient clang-clang of the motorman's bell; the wanderlust-evoking call of the steam-engine whistle on a hot summer night, spaced intermittently with the eerie sound of the home-brew bottle caps popping like howitzers all over the neighborhood; boys wearing straight knee pants and long black stockings (usually with a hole in one of the knees from playing marbles) through grade school, graduating to long pants when they started high school . . . the first 100-per-cent talking movies . . . and technocracy—the last of the T's and the glory of the A's . . . boys wearing their Scout knives on key rings and belt loops, which dangled in and out of their back pockets . . . making your first crystal radio set as soon as Mom emptied the rolled oatmeal box . . . emptying (and spilling) the wooden ice-box drip pan . . . the long-handled W.P.A. shovels and not a sign of a rabbit or a lone, lean male chasing a scrawny one . . . the Midwestern dust storms . . . the old variety store (near school) with the tall glass cases filled with penny stick candy . . . the penny postal and five-cent tram fare to the ball park . . . when the annual *Almanac* was gospel . . . how you forgot your number waiting for the phone operator . . . Rudy Vallee's "Hi-ho, everybody" . . . Ben Bernie, Husk O'Hare, and the great dance bands of the terrific twenties and thirties . . . how you had to play the cornet (or piano) for company . . . the gentle whir of the oscillating fan during the stifling heat of the dog days . . . gingerly running barefoot after the lumbering ice wagon . . . the baroque movie palaces with the mighty Wurlitzer and the hand-packed ice cream from the friendly corner drugstore . . . the long great superheterodynes with the curved speaker . . . when changing from "long-handles" to brief one-piece B.V.D.'s was one of the family's annual high points . . . plus fours and eights and bell-bottomed trousers along with F.D.R.'s fireside chats . . . our bakery: scrubbed, warm, tantalizingly aromatic and magical!

These are just a few of the heady scenes recalled of an Iowa boy's life spent in the rolling, lush plains and the lazy clay bluffs of not too long ago.

"Fifty years of age is not too long a time to learn one thing well— it takes centuries for a society to educate itself."

CONTENTS

"Mere knowledge is comparatively worthless unless digested into practical wisdom."—TRYON EDWARDS

INTRODUCTION

THE STAFF OF LIFE

The history of bread-baking is life itself—'tis the narrative of toil and sweat of the brow, the ceaseless struggle between soil and man. Wheat and bread created villages, communities, and nations; they helped to civilize the world. Christians and pagans alike believed wheat came from "above," the unleavened bread figured greatly in the lives of Jews and Christians alike. We now know that the Stone-Age housewife baked a "kind of bread," which was unleavened—truly the oldest of mankind's prepared foods.

The Egyptians baked the first known leavened bread in the first ovens and built a thriving industry. It has been told that all bread was unleavened until some absent-minded baker left the flat dough out in the air and warm sun, where it fermented. (Beer and yeast were discovered and produced by this same young Egyptian baker, so the story goes . . . Egyptians had good public relations—they invented long before the Russians.) The Romans "imported" many objects and people from Greece, including Greek bakers, the world's greatest of their day.

Thus began the closely governed baking profession-industry much as we know it today. . . A college of bakers was formed shortly after Christ's death . . . The common cry of "Bread and Circuses" was heard in the market places . . . Strict laws were imposed on bakers regarding the "social classes of bread"—senators' bread, nobles' bread, knights' bread, people's bread, peasants' bread, the bread varying from white to coarse dark, depending on the category. The quality and weight of each loaf were also strictly supervised. The baker milled his own flour until the Middle Ages, when the specialized miller moved near the streams to utilize the water power for his mills, and the baker remained close to his customers. Since all millers could not move to swift streams, they invented the windmill, but (weep for this modern man in olden days!) they were taxed out of business.

Bakers all over the world have an unwritten law, which was once an oath, to bake enough each day. "The baker's dozen" originated in the Middle Ages when the bakers who didn't abide by the oath, or short-weighed the bread, were beheaded in England and dunked in public in the Germanic provinces: hence the adding of one extra to each dozen!

Bakers became a well-respected lot, and community leaders. They worked hard as apprentices for three years, then as journeymen bakers for three to five years—or until age o'ertook the master baker and a vacancy appeared. As a journeyman baker, Dad baked and sold his loaves on the streets of Hamburg. At Yuletide the Tannenbaum Brot sold quickly in the holiday crowds, and the hot cross buns during Lent. The hours were long, and conditions poor at best, but the bakers were fiercely proud of their trade.

My father was the last of a long line of master bread bakers, and I'm sure that I almost broke his good heart by not following in his patient and knowing footsteps. Dad learned his trade (which was then a craft and an art, and is now a specialized science), as did all German lads, by the long, arduous, but thorough practice of apprenticing, working through grades of trade baker, until the day of realizing the ultimate: Master Bread Baker!

The priceless recipes presented in *Uncle John's Original Bread Book* have been handed down, family to family, baker to baker, friend to friend, tested and retested by Dad and thousands of unknowns—a dramatic living heritage—each one a part of our world history. Earlene and I are very proud of these recipes—and we know that my dear parents would wish to dedicate this book to the thousands of loyal friends and customers of Phoebe and Johann Braué of Council Bluffs, Iowa, and hinterlands; the scores of "log boys" who carried the long, heavy logs to the wood-burning oven for the delectable sweets that were their reward; the most co-operative railroad men of the Missouri Valley area, who carried the healthful breads and tasty baked goods to all parts of the country; the flour, bakery-supply, and yeast salesmen who were so helpful to the Braué Home Bakery; and to the numbers of persons who worked for my parents throughout the years.

The quotations sprinkled between recipes throughout the book are from the musty family files of the Rahns and the Braués. Most of them are from the minds of great men; others are just the author's musings.

We wish you many happy hours of baking!

BREAD-MAKING METHODS

There are four main operations, or methods, of preparing bread dough for baking:

THE SPONGE, OR LONG, METHOD. The yeast "works" with moisture, flour, and a few other ingredients, usually overnight, before being incorporated with the rest of the dough. Kneading and rising follow.

THE STRAIGHT DOUGH METHOD. All the ingredients are mixed, step by step, before the kneading and rising periods.

THE BATTER DOUGH METHOD. One mixing operation, with all ingredients, with no need for kneading and shaping (as liquids usually "outproportion" flour), and often only one rising period, after which dough is spread in pans or is spooned into tins.

THE NO-KNEAD METHOD. A thorough mixing operation, with no kneading, one rising period, and the dough is usually dropped or spooned into baking containers.

BREAD-MAKING-BAKING STEPS

MIXING. A thorough mixing, vigorously and confidently, is a definite must for the even distribution of the yeast cells and other ingredients. A prologue of flour blending helps too, and scalding the milk, dissolving the yeast or starter always precedes the mixing. Working the dough energetically by hand or with a wooden spoon is exercising and relaxing, pleasant too, with the "slooshing" sound of flour, and "clump-clumping" of spoon against bowl. But I am sure that most good readers will prefer the kitchen mixer. Please mix *thoroughly*.

KNEADING. This stretches the fabulous gluten into a minute elastic network and thoroughly blends the ingredients. Use a slightly floured board, table, pastry cloth, canvas—if lucky, a butcher's chopping block (table). When the dough becomes sticky (don't panic if you're a sticky mess), sprinkle the working surface with a little flour—not too much, though, as a heavy batch (dough) results in slower rising and a coarser-textured bread. Oily hands will help. Knead until the dough is satiny-smooth and "alive." (You can see the small bubbles under the dough's skin.) Let it rest for a few seconds; then roll the dough into a ball, place it in a greased bowl, turn over once (or oil top of dough), and cover with a clean cloth.

RISING. Allow the yeast to act, for good texture and flavor, in a draftless spot at 83° to 90° F.—never too cool or too warm. A humid-proof box is the ideal place to let the home-made bread "rise in favor," but there are also other methods: cover with a clean cloth, damp or dry, waxed paper or a glass bowl; place the bowl of dough in the oven over a pan of hot water; or set the bowl in a pan of hot water, or on the hot-water heater, a radiator, the TV set (while you watch your show), warmed bricks or a heating pad. As Aunt Chick advises, try the hot sun on a calm day. Whatever your favorite warming place (the more humid the better), to test for correct rising time, press two fingers, or knuckles, deeply into the risen dough. If the dents remain and bubbles shyly present themselves for their popping good time, then follow the next step of the recipe.

SHAPING OR MOLDING. After the dough has experienced its final rising, cut it into equal portions and roll them into balls. Well-worked dough may be molded and shaped to your will. Use either the hand or the rolling-pin method. If by hand, flatten the dough into a rectangle and press out all bubbles; fold first one long side over to the center, then the other, so that they overlap. Roll the dough into a loaf, sealing and tucking under the inner edge. Place in a greased pan with the seam side at the bottom. If using a rolling pin, roll and flatten the dough into a rectangle; then roll the dough like a jelly roll, starting at one of the narrower sides of the rectangle and sealing the inner edge. Seal the ends and edges, and place in a greased pan seam side down. For a softer crust, brush the tops of the loaves with shortening (oil or butter) after baking. For a glazy-crispy crust, brush the tops of the loaves with a mixture of egg white and water before baking.

BAKING. Baking stops the rising process, induces a pleasant waft of fragrance, sets the conditioned gluten, and makes for flavorful bread. Thoroughly baked breads are golden brown, pull away slightly from the sides of the baking pans, and sound hollow to the tap of knuckles on the crusty top. The loaves should tumble from the pans to cool on a wire rack.

Now comes the hardest job of all: keeping the bread from the family until it has cooled! Cut hot, fresh bread with a pre-heated serrated (saw-toothed) knife. A crisp crust calls for neither greasing the tops of loaves nor covering the loaves as they cool; soft crust calls for lightly greasing tops and covering loaves with a cloth as they cool, but only for a few minutes.

Cool the loaves completely before placing them in a bread box, plastic bags, or foil. Bread will keep very well in your freezer if wrapped in moisture-proof plastics or foil.

EATING. The proof of the mix: the proud moment as you watch your family demolish your bread!

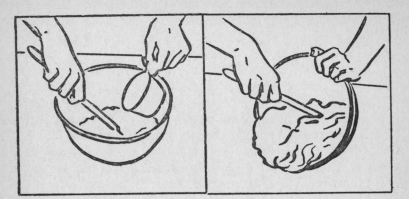

After dissolving the yeast in liquid, stir in about half the flour. Beat until smooth. Mix the dough until it rolls from the sides of the bowl.

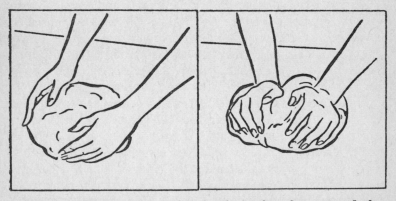

With floured hands, shape the dough for kneading. Knead the dough by pressing it flat, then folding the dough over on itself toward you. Then push away from you with the heels of your hands. Give the dough a quarter turn, fold, and push again. Relax and enjoy this with your favorite waltz for at least five minutes— a push, a turn—until the dough feels as soft as a baby's skin.

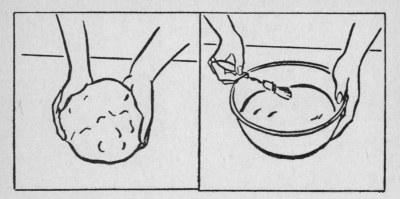

Let the dough rest for a second. Then shape it for rising. Place the dough in a greased bowl. Turn it over once, or grease the top of the dough. Let it rise.

The dough should rise until doubled in bulk. Test it by pressing two fingers into it. If the "hole-presses" remain, the dough has risen. "Punch inna da dough . . ." Pull the dough away from the sides of the bowl; center it. Turn it out onto a floured board, and shape it into a ball.

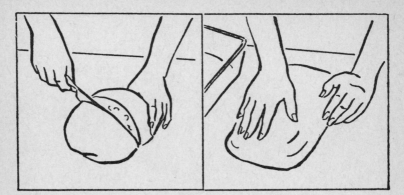

Cut the dough with a sharp knife for rolls. Let pieces of dough rest a bit. For a beautiful, shapely loaf, stretch and pat out the

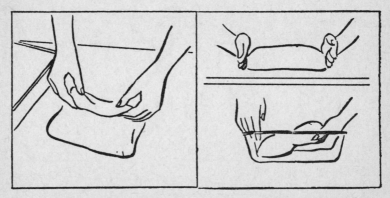

dough into an oblong oval. Press out the gas bubbles; then fold it lengthwise, edges into the center. Pinch the edges together. Roll and place the sealed edges downward in a bread pan.

GOOD BAKING TOOLS

standard measuring cups and spoons (for dry and liquid measure)
wooden mixing spoon, paddle, and bowl
slotted mixing spoon
scoop(s)
rubber scraper
steel bowl knife, cutting knives, dough chopper or cutter
egg beater
wire whisk
flour sifter and small sieves
mixing bowls with sloping sides and round bottoms
well-acquainted baking pans and other containers of all sorts and sizes
pastry brush and blender
biscuit cutter
wire racks (preferably with legs, for air circulation)
baking thermometers (candy, oven, baking-cooking)
scissors
topping decorator (a plastic squeeze bottle will do nicely)
cake tester (or wooden toothpick or broom straw)
kneading surface
electric mixer (follow directions carefully, remembering the difference between spoon and mixer mixing)
an oven you love (or at least know well)

. . . though actually the basics are the oven, a large mixing bowl, a wooden board or table, a mixing spoon, a measuring cup, bread pans (standard 9 by 5 by 3 inches), a large cover-all apron—clean, willing arms and hands.

"Home-baked bread is healthful and honest."
—PHOEBE *und* JOHANN BRAUÉ

A FEW NATURAL SAVORY INGREDIENTS RECOMMENDED FOR TANTALIZING MIXING

carob powder (St.-John's-bread, Boecksur, locust bean, or honey locust)
fruits of all kinds (fresh, dried, or frozen)
lemon and orange peels (grated or powdered)
cooked porridge (old-fashioned porridge or cooked cereal of your choice)
cereals
soybeans, lentils, sweet and white potatoes (all cooked or puréed)
sunflower-seed meal
soy and corn grits
rice polishings
chopped nuts
grated cheese
eggs (raw, dried)
fruit juice
carrots and some soups
soaked and sprouted whole grains
berries
honey
nutritional yeast
unhydrogenated oils
soy lecithin spread
wheat germ

. . . and the wonderful romantic world of spices now encompassing the colorful and varied herbs, salts, and seeds, plus the historical spices, categorically:

SPICES: allspice, cayenne, cinnamon, cloves, ginger, mace, nutmeg, paprika, black pepper, white pepper, red pepper, saffron (more better in this group), tumeric

AROMATIC SEEDS: anise, caraway, cardamom, celery, coriander, cumin, dill, fennel, fenugreek, mustard, poppy

HERBS: basil, bay leaves, chervil, marjoram, mint, oregano, parsley, rosemary, sage, savory, tarragon, thyme

BLENDS OF SPICES: chili powder, curry powder, fines herbes, mixed pickling spice, poultry seasoning, pumpkin-pie spice

SEASONING SALTS: celery salt, garlic salt, onion salt . . . the list is endless.

"He hath good judgment that relieth not wholly on his own."

HEALTHFUL HINTS ON BAKING

Baking skill is acquired through practice—you do not have to be a born baker or have a special talent. Doing a good job over and over again, as we instruct our own children, will bring about a satisfying result. You too can be an artist—create and your results will live. There are no real "tricks to the trade," just a few rules to follow:

Plan, be prepared, have all tools and ingredients at hand, have a good work area. Pick out a recipe, read it through once, read it again, carefully—understand all of the preparation steps clearly. Make sure that all ingredients and utensils are at room temperature. (Rinse utensils in hot water.) Use standard measuring spoons and cups—all measurements are level.

You may not love your oven; at least be well acquainted with it; preheat it and check the evenness of the temperature. Bake in the center of the oven (not cool at one side and hot at the other).

Fresh flour is best stored in a cool spot.

You can always fit bread-making into your busy schedule—late at night mix the whole batch and place it in the refrigerator; the moisture will help the gluten. Early in the morning, or during the day between your favorite programs and appointments, you can bake. Make sure the dough is always stiff enough to handle, and not too sticky. Rewash your hands, reflour them—or grease them, for dark breads. Exact measurements for flour and exact time for kneading are seldom given in these recipes, but you will learn good consistency of yeast doughs in jig time. You will discover new variations in flour. Patience will bring praise from family and friends.

We were not meant to live on bread alone, but we could, healthfully, with organically grown, stone-ground, unbleached flours. (Yes, the milling of whole grains is almost a lost art.) There is nothing more satisfying to the home cook than producing a perfect loaf of bread. 'Tis superior therapy, an adventure in the kitchen that will never grow tedious. "Try and err," but you will win, if you experiment—ever patient—for the kneading, rising, and baking of bread is the making of a miracle. . . .

When Dad was selling a pound loaf of bread for a nickel, he and the Iowa farmers were predicting that, as the price of bread rose, the farmers' dollar share would drop.

To reheat bread or rolls, preheat the oven to 400° F. Turn the oven off. Sprinkle a paper bag with water, place baked goods in the bag, then put in the oven for about ten minutes.

If you use self-rising flour, omit salt. Self-rising flour is flour + leavening agent.

Dough rises best at from 80° to 86° F., in an undrafty spot. Use an accurate thermometer for predictable results. Keep the dough covered while it rises to glorious heights; *never* let it chill.

Climatic conditions play Ned with ovens, so please try, try again. Bake at 380° to 480° F. for 10 to 15 minutes; then reduce oven temperature to 350° F. for the remainder of 1 hour. Loaves of medium size should bake 45 to 50 minutes; larger loaves take 1 hour or more. Just don't say "can't," *richtig*?

Baking temperatures for yeast breads go from the moderate 350° F. to the hot 450° F. When baking with earthenware, use the lower shelf of the oven at 50° F. below the usual baking temperature.

Lower temperatures are used for the rich roll doughs.

Try coffee cans for sweet yeast-dough baking.

When using glass loaf pans, the oven should be 25° F. less than usual, to prevent thick crusts. Bake a few loaves in casserole dishes—round, long, large or small; try the silicone plastic-coated wax pans. But keep all bread and dough utensils clinically clean!

A friend of mine says that his Italian baker used to have a musical swing to his punching the sponge: "Punch inna da dough; fold inna da punch; heel inna da dough . . ." Try it with your overnight sponge. This will work especially well with the second rising, as it will improve the flavor and texture of the bread.

My parents' suggestions for home-freezing of breads:

UNBAKED. Before the last rising, wrap the bread dough in moisture-vapor-proof material and secure tightly; then place in freezer. The dough should be used for baking within a week or ten days from the time of freezing. The night before the dough is to be used, transfer it to the refrigerator for even, overnight defrosting, because room temperature would produce uneven rising (icy inside, rising outside). In the good morning, knead as usual, even though the dough is soggy. Then let rise and bake.

BAKED. Wrap the loaf tightly in moisture-vapor-proof material and place in freezer. It may be stored for weeks, but not more than three months. When ready to eat, defrost for at least two to three hours at room temperature. Frozen bread, baked and unbaked, seems to have a more pronounced bread taste.

I read somewhere not too long ago the crowning blow. We have been taught and commanded to eat all of the bread, as the crust is supposed to be the most nourishing portion. Now we learn that American astronauts are fed bread *without* crusts! I would like to speak with their dietician. (I understand that a few astronauts enjoy onion dark bread too.)

"Holes in bread? Ja wohl! Yust not too big."

A BRIEF GLOSSARY OF BAKING TERMS

Add. To spoon, pour, etc., further dry or liquid ingredients to a mixture, then to stir it in.

Bake. To cook in covered or uncovered containers in any type of oven.

Batch. From sponge to dough.

Batter. Any mixture of flour, moisture, and other ingredients.

Beat. To thoroughly stir, blend or beat with hands, spoon or mixer.

Blanch. To dip food first into boiling water, then into cold.

Blend. To mix two or more ingredients thoroughly.

Boil. To cook in a liquid hot enough for bubbles to rise and break on the surface (like swimmers popping up after a dive).

Caramelize. To heat sugar slowly, or a mixture containing sugar, until it is brown and flavorful.

Combine. To introduce and mix ingredients.

Consistency. Thoroughly incorporated, but not overmixed.

Cream. To work one or more combinations until creamy soft.

Cut. To incorporate shortening with dry ingredients, using a fork, knife, or a blender.

Dissolve. To combine dry and liquid ingredients (yeast + liquid, etc.).

Dock. To punch loaves, before baking, with a clean nail or knife.

Dot. To toss on top of dough or another mixture.

Dough. A mixture of flour or meal and liquid stiff enough to handle.

Dredge. To coat with flour or sugar.

Dust. To sprinkle lightly with flour or sugar.

Fold. To combine ingredients or two mixtures with a spatula, a slotted spoon, or a whisk, using a gentle "down, across the bottom of the mixture, up and over" action until well blended.

Incorporate. To blend in thoroughly.

Knead. To rhythmically press, stretch, and fold dough over on itself, and pushing with the palms of the hands.

Make stiff. To add enough flour to dough to realize a thorough mix.

Make up. To mold dough into loaves.

Proof. To let dough rise in a humid spot (in pantry or on shelf).

Purée. To force-strain through a sieve for even consistency.

Recover. To let dough recoup some of its former strength and life—"rest and recover."

Render. To melt fat from other tissue.

Reserve. To save or set aside "for another day."

Rest. To leave dough "for a spell"—"rest and recover," a resting period.

Round up. To roll into a ball before making into loaves.

Roux. A thickening mixture of fat and flour (common preparation in European cooking and baking).

Sauté. To cook or brown in a small amount of fat. (Two schools of thought: quickly, or over low heat?)

Scald. To heat liquid *just below* the boiling point (until the surface is puckery).

Scale. To weigh dough before making it up into loaves.

Score. To make a series of shallow cuts on the surface of dough.

Simmer. To cook in a liquid held just below its boiling point, so that the bubbles break below the surface.

Slash. To cut the tops of loaves, before baking, diagonally with a sharp knife or razor blade.

Sour (saur) starter. A preparatory sponge.

Sponge. Batter to which yeast or starter has been added.

Spoon in. To add to a mixture with a spoon, then stir.

Spread. To cover a surface evenly with a substance by using a knife or spatula.

Steam. To cook in steam, with or without pressure, in a covered container.

Stew and stock. To simmer-boil in liquid (broth).

Stir in. To mix in with a circular motion with a mixer or a spoon.

Toss. To mix with a fork (and/or a spoon), lifting lightly and often.

Turn out. To move dough or bread out of a container.
Whip. To beat vigorously with a wire whisk or rotary beater.
Work in. To incorporate ingredients thoroughly into a batter.

A FEW WEIGHTS, MEASURES AND EQUIVALENTS

A pinch	= a bit more than barely between thumb and forefinger
glug-glug	= depends on family traditions; Earlene's family believes in big glug-glugs
dash	= less than ⅛ teaspoon (hmmm, I've seen it go over ½ teaspoon in G.I. kitchens!)
60 drops	= 1 teaspoon
3 teaspoons	= 1 tablespoon
4 tablespoons	= ¼ cup
4 cups	= 1 quart
2 tablespoons butter	= 1 ounce (lard, margarine, fat)
2 tablespoons liquid	= 1 ounce
1 cup liquid	= ½ pound
2 cups solid shortening	= 1 pound (remember "lard or country butter the size of a walnut"?)
1 cup sugar	= a bit less than a cup of honey, syrup or sorghum
2 + cups granulated sugar	= 1 pound
2⅔ cups brown sugar	= 1 pound
1 square bitter chocolate	= 1 ounce

2½ cups powdered sugar	= 1 pound
3½ cups confectioners' sugar	= 1 pound
1 cup	= ½ pint; 8 fluid ounces; 16 tablespoons
2 pints	= 1 quart
4 quarts	= 1 gallon (liquid)
4 quarts	= 1 peck (solid)
4 pecks	= 1 bushel (here are two items slowly leaving the market scene)
16 ounces	= 1 pound
1 medium egg	= 2 ounces
8–10 medium eggs	= 1 pound
5 medium eggs	= 1 cup
8–10 egg whites	= 1 cup
12–14 egg yolks	= 1 cup
4 cups all-purpose flour, sifted	= 1 pound
4½ cups cake or pastry flour, sifted	= 1 pound
3½ cups rye or whole-wheat flour, unsifted	= 1 pound
3 cups cornmeal or oatmeal	= 1 pound
1 cake compressed yeast	= 1 package active dry yeast
1 ounce active dry yeast	= 4 tablespoons

On "jibbles and shmidgeons," 'tis the cook's upbringing.

Cans

8-ounce	= 1 cup	No. 2	= 2½ cups
Picnic	= 1¼ cups	No. 3 squat	= 2¾ cups
12-ounce	= 1⅔ cups	No. 2½	= 3½ cups
No. 300	= 1¾ cups	No. 3	= 4 cups
No. 1 tall	= 2 cups	No. 5	= 7¼ cups
No. 303	= 2 cups	No. 10	= 13 cups

Home-made bread is yummy-good; and it is just a question of being near the kitchen—first to mix, then to knead, now to shape, finally to bake to a golden brown.

Oven Temperatures

Very slow	250–275° F.
Slow	300–325° F.
Moderate	350–375° F.
Hot	400–425° F.
Very hot	450–475° F.
Extremely hot	500–525° F.

THE BASIC INGREDIENTS

My Deutsche father used to say, oh, so many times, "*Nu, nu,* Johann, fvrom der pbeginning, *ja, Junge?*" So from the beginning of the living history of bread we present the joys of making-baking good bread, mixing your own batch with the variables of yeast, liquids, and flour, plus the right ingredients—realizing the results of your own judgment.

The two general classes of breads are quick and yeast breads.

QUICK BREADS. Leavened with baking powder, soda, air, sourdough starters, or steam—such as biscuits, muffins, corn and spoon breads, nut-fruit breads, griddle cakes, doughnuts, popovers, and the fancylike. They rarely require the rising, kneading, and shaping of yeast breads, but must be mixed thoroughly, and can be served in a flash of a guest's notice.

YEAST BREADS. Leavened with yeast (or starters, etc.) and prepared by the sponge method or straight dough process—dot iss, whole-wheat, white, pumpernickel, rye, *und so weiter*—and must be mixed, kneaded, risen, shaped, baked, eaten or stored . . .

"Much virtue in herbs, not much in men."

YEAST. Yeast is a living plant mass that thrives on warmth (80–85° F.) and moisture, and is responsible for the fermentation of the dough. The two preparations of yeast available for home baking are active dry yeast and compressed yeast. Yeast *must* be fresh, and always dissolved in moisture; it will be utterly destroyed by high or low temperatures. *Active dry yeast* is in a dormant state and will keep very well in a cool, dry place; it comes to life when dissolved with warm water, 105–115° F. *Compressed yeast* is alive and most perishable—should not be stored in refrigerator more than a week. It is moist, grayish, and almost odorless when fresh, and is best dissolved in lukewarm water 80–90° F.

The yeast causes the dough to rise and become porous; usually one or two packages of active dry yeast (or cakes) are used with six to eight cups of flour. Rich doughs require more yeast; overnight sponges require less. Your friendly neighborhood baker may give or sell you a "thumb" of his bakers' yeast.

MOISTURE. Liquids used may be a single or combination of liquids or stocks. The popular usuals are water, milk (excellent in any form), potato water. Milk and potato water should be scalded in the top of a double boiler, then cooled to correctness before the yeast is added. Test temperature as you would a baby's bottle, wrist-like. Just plain water presents a crusty-crisp loaf with a homey wheat taste. Potato water keeps the bread moist and quickens the "working" of the yeast. Milk produces a softer, creamier, mellow-texture loaf.

HEAT. A warm, cozy kitchen, ingredients, and utensils will result in the finest of bread. The temperature should be between 75° and 85° F. (preferably 80°). Oven-warm everything and test by thermometer or wrist method. (If no warmth or coolness is felt, 'tis good.)

SUGAR. This is the "spur," from which the yeast produces the leavening (food for the yeast). It aids in the golden-browning and flavoring of the bread.

SALT. The "bridle," which controls the fermentation (rising), and gives flavor. 'Tis life-giving.

SHORTENING. Gluten's neighborly body builder (helps dough

to expand evenly and smoothly), makes the bread flavorful and tender-rich. The most commonly used shortenings are lards, fats, oils, butter, margarine. For a tender mixture and downright good flavor, Dad mixed butter and hydrogenated shortening together. (For rendering lard, see page 191.)

FLOUR. The chief ingredient in bread is the flour that you will use in your mix, and it must be *top grade!* The basic grain is wheat, which, when milled, produces the gluten which stretches to form a netlike texture that holds the bubbles formed by the "working" of the yeast. There are two general kinds of wheat flour—hard-wheat flour and soft-wheat flour. Hard-wheat-flour doughs have more elasticity; this flour makes grainy, large loaves and demands more liquids. It is used mostly in making

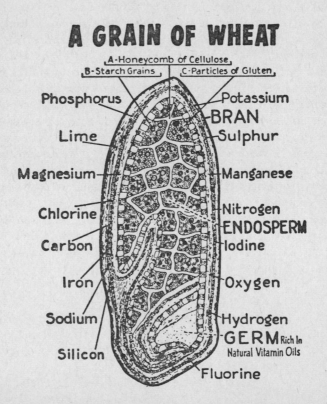

A GRAIN OF WHEAT

A-Honeycomb of Cellulose
B-Starch Grains
C-Particles of Gluten

Phosphorus — Potassium
BRAN
Lime — Sulphur
Magnesium — Manganese
Chlorine — Nitrogen
ENDOSPERM
Carbon — Iodine
Iron — Oxygen
Sodium — Hydrogen
GERM Rich In Natural Vitamin Oils
Silicon
Fluorine

yeast breads. Soft-wheat flours have less elasticity and are more delicate. This flour makes smaller, fine-grained loaves and is often used in making pies, cakes, and quick breads. You may prefer the all-purpose (family) flour or the new quick flours in all your baking. Enriched flour, briefly, is the milled inner portion of the wheat, to which iron and vitamin B have been added.

We heartily and healthfully recommend the "biblical" seven grain flours—wheat, corn, barley, oat, rye, soybean, and rice— for making interesting bread. There are many others—bulghur (kasha, or parched wheat), buckwheat, oatmeal, millet, cottonseed, peanut, graham, and bran. Such an appealing list with which to experiment—all with more than a hint of flavor and taste. And the list goes on; try the honest stone-ground flours in all your mixes. 'Tis the entire wholesome grain freshly ground to flour, possessing the flavorsome, nutritional wheat germ.

Whole-wheat and graham flours, possessing most of the bran of the wheat, must be blended with white flour, or the dough will be too sticky to knead. Rye flour, the versatile knight of the bread round table, nearly like wheat, will not harbor the starter or yeast; szto a sponge is therefore prepared from wheat flour, developing the yeast and gluten for the addition of the hard-to-handle rye flour.

Forget your timidity. Blend your flours for pleasurable excitement! The actual baking characteristics of flour vary with the climate, altitude, seasons, soil, type of wheat, milling, storage conditions, moisture absorption, and many other factors, so please contact your home demonstration agent and your utilities dietician for invaluable assistance.

"Bread making is first likened to an old German band—a cacaphony—then the completeness of a symphony—a perfect blend of good ingredients and interpretation—completely satisfying."

JOHANN BRAUÉ, *Artist and good father.*

"I do the very best I know how—the very best I can—and I mean to keep on doing so until the end."

—ABRAHAM LINCOLN (General MacArthur's goal)

Ferment and Leavening

"What the superior man seeks in himself; what the small man seeks in others."—CONFUCIUS

"Luck is in direct proportion to preparation, hard work, and opportunity."—Written on tablets of jade somewhere

SODA AND BAKING POWDER

Sponges, starters, batters, doughs, and other types of mixes are the usual forms in which flour is used as a basic ingredient. A thin batter equals 1 measure of liquid plus 1½ measures of flour. Drop dough equals 1 measure of liquid to 2 measures of flour. A stiff dough equals 1 measure of liquid to 3 measures of flour.

A leavening other than yeast or baking powder is produced when soda is heated to neutralize the acid of sour milk or molasses. The gas that is formed from this is not as easily controlled, nor is the amount sufficient to produce complete leavening power.

A rule for using soda:

> 1 teaspoon soda
> 2 cups completely soured milk

A rule for using baking powder:

1 level teaspoon baking powder to each level cup of flour—for bread or quick breads, or cake-baking

1½ level teaspoons baking powder to each level cup of bread flour

Confederate housewives used corncob ash to make dough rise!

"The ideal diet is that combination of food which, while imposing the least burden upon the body, supplies it with exactly sufficient material to meet its wants."—SCHUSTER

YEAST AND STARTERS

Yeast has served the world in a most mysterious manner since the time of the ancients, especially in the making of bread and beer. A sour-dough leavening was reserved for each baking batch. Spanish beauties of centuries ago even used the fermentation for facial treatment. Not until Pasteur did we begin to get a clear understanding of the true nature of yeast. Its contribution to human welfare has been fantastic.*

Dad's Saxon Yeast

Become an expert with the following.

4 oz. hops
4 quarts water
4 pounds rye flour (or meal)

8 pounds barley flour
6 oz. yeast (bakers' or packaged) (or 3 cups starter)

Boil hops in water for 30 minutes. Strain into a large mixing bowl and set aside until the mixture has cooled to warm. Add rye flour or rye meal to the mixture, mix well, then add yeast and mix thoroughly. Place the mixture in a moderately warm room to stand overnight; the following morning should find this mass in a state of fermentation.

Add the barley flour to the fermented mixture. Mix to form a dough. Roll out and cut into thin disks. Dry in the open air, away from the sun, and break into small pieces for immediate

---

* Two interestingly informative booklets on yeast may be had for the asking by writing to W. A. Hardwick, Director, Fermentation Section, Central Research Department, Anheuser-Busch, Inc., St. Louis, Missouri; and to Leonard M. Gocek, National Yeast Corporation, 800 Mill Street, Belleville, New Jersey. Uncle John's Dry Sour-Dough Starter is available, postpaid $1.00, from Uncle John, P.O. Box 3276, Midland, Texas 79704.

use, remembering that 1 tablespoon equals 1 cake or package of yeast.

To preserve the yeast, follow this process:

Crumble the disks and thoroughly dry them (on absorbent paper away from the sun). Then package in moderately airtight containers for long-time preservation in a cool place. (Do not freeze.)

When adding the yeast to hops-rye mixture, mix the yeast in a small portion of the mixed flours, then add that to the rest of the hops-rye mixture. Hops are obtainable at your favorite druggist or wholesale drug house. Yeast is found in the grocery store or bakery. Various flours are stocked in health-food stores.

Dad's Schleswig-Holstein Farmer's Yeast

An early savings account.

2 packages active dry yeast (or 2 cups starter)	1 quart water, boiling
	1 cup hops, with pollen
1 cup water, warm	1 teaspoon salt
6 medium-size potatoes, pared and cubed	1 cup honey
	4 cups whole-wheat flour

Dissolve the yeast in 1 cup warm water. Stir and mix the boiling water, hops, and potatoes in a large pot. Cover and simmer until the potatoes are tender. Strain out the hops. Purée the potatoes. Add and mix enough of the flour to make a thick batter along with the salt and honey. Stir well while you gradually heat to boiling point. Remove mixture from heat and cool to lukewarm. Add the dissolved yeast and stir easily. Cover and let stand at room temperature until light and spongy. Use as needed, and reserve in a loosely covered scalded jar or "sotz crock." Keep in refrigerator; do *not* freeze.

"Isn't it great? We can blame our fathers for the wars and depressions and know that it'll all be paid for by our children and their heirs!"

Yeast Cakes

Through the kindness of Mrs. Charles Vanderford of Midland, Texas, her good mother, and an old friend, here's another live helper in the kitchen.

¼ cup hops
1 cup water
1 medium-size potato
water to cover

¼ cup flour
½ cup corn meal
corn meal for dipping

Place ¼ cup hops in a pan and cover with 1 cup water. Let this come to a boil, reduce heat, and simmer 20 minutes with lid on pan. It should yield ½ cup hops water after straining.

Peel and slice the potato into another pot. Use just enough water to cover and boil until well done. Drain; it should yield 1 cup of potato liquid.

Mix hops water and potato liquid, and while still hot, pour over ¼ cup flour and ½ cup corn meal, making a stiff paste.

Let cool; then roll into cakes, using 2 tablespoons of paste for each cake. Dip cakes in corn meal and roll until easily handled.

Dry for several days on wire rack, turning daily. They may be used immediately, but they must be *perfectly dry* before storing in a cool place or the refrigerator. Yield: 16 cakes.

"Memory is the mother of all wisdom."—AESCHYLUS

Yeast Patties

A combination of the good points of the recipes of Mrs. Vanderford and Dad.

2 cups starter (or a pkg. of active dry yeast)
5 cups warm water
5 tablespoons shortening
5 tablespoons sugar (or honey, molasses, or syrup)

1 tablespoon salt
4 cups flour (rye—dark or white)
¼ teaspoon ginger
some corn meal

In a warm crock, mix the first six ingredients to a thin batter. Cover and let rise, overnight, in a warm place.

The next morning, reserve one cup for future starter, or for current bread-baking. For the yeast patties, stir into the overnight mixture ¼ teaspoon ginger, enough corn meal to make a stiff dough, and stir well. Pat into small, round patties (cookie style), place on a sheet to dry, and turn them every day.

"Remember when the glory of work was work itself?—its own reward."

Dad's Yeast-Starter Mixture

½ pound hops	½ pound fine malt flour
1 gallon water	½ pound brown sugar

As Dad used to say, *"Ja wohl,* to pbegin der yeast . . ."

In one gallon of water boil the hops for half an hour. Strain and stir in the malt flour. Then strain this mixture through a coarse cloth and boil for about 10 minutes.

Let the mixture rest until lukewarm, then stir in the brown sugar.

Remove mixture to a jug and keep in a warm place for working. Cap tightly and store in a cool place for future baking use.

"Care to our coffin adds a nail, no doubt,
And every grin, so merry, draws one out."—JOHN WOLCOT

Dad's On-the-Trail Yeast

Used by many a trail cook, Mormon, and prospector.

Boil, skin, and mash mealy potatoes in the potato water. Stir in molasses, sugar, salt, hops, and unbleached flour. Bring to boil, stirring the while; boil for a bit, then remove to crock to cool. Use and reserve.

"There is nothing stronger and nobler than when man and wife are of one heart and mind in a house, a grief to their foes, and to their friends great joy, but their own hearts know it best."
—HOMER

Dad's Rahn-Braué Starter Mixture

**Carried by my father, in a jar, from Deutschland to America—
will work very well with quick breads too.**

3 large, clean, sound potatoes   2 cups cold water
2 cups water, boiling   1 cup starter, or
2 tablespoons salt   1 package active dry yeast,
4 tablespoons honey   dissolved in warm water

Pare and cut potatoes into small pieces, and cook until tender
in boiling water. Mash potatoes in the water in which they were
cooked, then add, stirring, the honey, salt, and enough of the
cold water to make about 4 cups of liquid.

Set aside until lukewarm; then add the starter (or dissolved
yeast), stir, and allow this mixture to stand overnight, covered.

In the morning the mixture should greet you "foamingly
light." Stir well; pour off 1 cup for baking, and reserve the rest
in a clean, loosely covered jar placed in a cool place or in the
refrigerator. *Do not freeze.* No spoilage will result if used often

"Satisfying fault doubles it."—French proverb

SOUR DOUGH

"Sourdough" was the name attached to Alaskan prospectors or Canadian foresters because these pioneers carried the valuable possession, wild yeast, sour dough, with them in a lump for making bread while camping. Sour dough is an "invaluable clump" of dough kept in a closed jar or crock and containing a living and continuing fermentation.

"He who dies for virtue does not perish."—PLAUTUS

Grandmother's Sour-Dough Starter
Our matriarch's historical leavening.

4 potatoes
water
4 cups rye flour (or rye meal, or regular flour)

½ cup honey (or 2 tablespoons sugar)
2 teaspoons salt

Boil 4 clean, solid potatoes in clear water (with jackets on). Remove 2 potatoes, peel; mash potatoes in water they were boiled in.

Mix with about 4 cups of rye flour (or meal, or just plain flour), at least ¼ cup honey (or 2 tablespoons sugar), and 2 teaspoons salt.

Remove to large crock, cover, and let stand in warm spot for nearly 4 days (until bubbly and odoriferous!). Reserve for required use. (Yeast will hurry the fermentation process.)

"He that asketh faintly beggeth a denial."—FULLER

Dad's German Sour-Dough Starter

Also brought to this country by my father in a jar . . . "worth its volume in gold."

·1 cup starter (or 1 pkg. dry yeast)
2 cups warm water
2 cups rye flour (or 1½ cups rye meal)

Thoroughly mix 1 cup of starter (or 1 package dry yeast) with 2 cups of warm water and 2 cups of rye flour (or 1½ cups of rye meal), stirring easily.

Place in crock, cover, and keep at room temperature for 3 days, letting it rise and fall while reaching the sourness you wish. Then incorporate thoroughly with your desired bread-dough mix.

Reserve 1 cup for future use.

"Think long when you may decide only once."—PUBLIUS SYRUS

Mother's Sour Starter

An unusually simple and active helper.

1 cup milk   1 cup flour

Place milk in a glass jar or crock and let it stand for 24 hours at room temperature. Stir in 1 cup flour (rye *der bestes*, but any type is accepted).

Leave mixture uncovered in a warm place for 3 days, or until bubbly and sour.

"Friendship is the bond of reason."—SHERIDAN

Ash Leavening

Good farm and hill folk the world over have used this with varied results.

Mix hardwood ashes with boiling water. Let ash settle, and use liquid as baking soda.

Hasten Jasen Sour-Dough Starter

Mix 1 quart flour (unbleached, rye, or dark), 1 teaspoon salt, and 2 tablespoons sugar with enough warm water to make a fairly thick batter. (A grated Irish potato or a bit of yeast will help the fermentation.) Let stand for 1 day. Reserve most; use a bit for a sponge.

"Eat it up, wear it out, make it do, or go without."—Yankee thrift

Malt-Hops Mixin'

Boil malt and hops in water. Let stand for 24 hours (der nacht und tag). Let it dry in sun. Use as yeast crumbles.

"Distrust is poison to friendship."

Malt Blend

Boil 2 parts malt in 3 parts water. Set aside half the mixture in a crock in a warm place for a day and a night. With the other half repeat the process and add to original mixture until there is enough yeast for a baking and a starter.

"Nothing is worth so much as a mind well instructed."—The Bible

Corn-Meal–Hops Yeast

Best when hops are plucked right from vine and put in outside boiling vat.

Pour water over hops in boiling container until almost covered. Bring to boil; boil 3 minutes. Drain off liquor while it is still hot. Stir in enough white or yellow corn meal to thicken. Spread the mixture on cloth or a board to dry.

"Vision is the art of seeing things invisible."—SWIFT

My Uncle John's Grain Yeast

Grind to a powder, and blend, equal parts of Indian corn, barley, and rye—all sprouting. Mix with water and boil to a good thick mess. Let stand for a day. Remove globules from the surface and use now. Dry the remainder and reserve.

In the making of yeast, you former home brewers possessed some mighty fine formulas, nicht wahr? Yeast is added to starters to quicken fermentation. No, no "jungle juicers"—dried fruit, sugar and water is too "raunchy!"

Bits of Dough

The convenience of this age of instant everything in our modern home living far outweighs the hope of the return of the traditional "bread day" of our yesteryears; but what stirring memories! The golden-brown, crusty-good loaves of home-made bread that graced the kitchens of our mothers and grandmothers belong to generations past—this heavenly aroma that permeated homes and human beings and happily told us, with a delicious exclamation point, that taste-tempting yeast breads were being created in the lived-in kitchens. Szo ledt's try some "instant living" and recapture some of the pleasurable nostalgia of the magical days of our mothers and grandmothers and live a whole new life of culinary adventures: the baking of this honorable and ancient food—bread! You will be affectionately rewarded in enthusiastic response; your joy of accomplishment will be unmatched!

The following limited words are "bread upon the waters" lovingly placed for your ultimate pleasure—the fulfillment of a dream translated from old script, Deutsche (curdled by a Midwestern accent), Pennsylvania Dutch (Pumpernickel Wilhelm) . . . volume baking to kitchen size, and just plain hand-me-down treasures.

"Wise crumbs that falleth thy way."—MOTHER *and* DADDY

Quick Breads

*"What hymns are sung, what praises said,
For homemade miracles of bread?"*

—Louis Untermeyer

SAVORY QUICK BREADS

Christmas with the Braués and the Rahns was completely wrapped up in wholesome tradition, and we hope to impart some of the surprises of the baked gifts to you.

"The secret of success is constancy to purpose."—DISRAELI

Mutter Phoebe's Date-Nut Bread

A reminder, a bit, of Boston brown bread, eh, Mother—the baking, that is. A favorite of Mother's friends around the holidays.

½ pound pitted dates, up cutten
2 teaspoons baking soda
2 cups boiling water
¼ cup shortening (or butter, margarine, oil)
2 cups sugar
2 eggs, beaten slightly

2 teaspoons salt
1 cup nut meats, up der choppen
4 cups all-purpose flour (a mixture of your favorite flours—soya, unbleached, graham, white)

Combine dates, soda, den der boilingk vater over pour. Set aside to cool, while, in another bowl, cream together sugar, butter, and eggs. Blend flour and salt into date mixture, stir well while you mix in the nut meats, until glistening-smooth.

Spoon into 6 #303 cans (greased, with wax-paper circle on bottom of each can), fill each can half full, and bake in dry or moist 325° F. oven for 1 hour. Slide bread out to rack or bread board and slice with cheese slicer, or cord "lassoed" around loaf, sharply pulled.

Bake up ahead of holidays, and freezer geputten.

"The more noble, the more humble."

Rahn-Braué Honey Cakes

Lebkuchen wunderbar!

½ teaspoon soda
1 teaspoon cinnamon
1 teaspoon ginger
1 teaspoon ground cloves
1 teaspoon nutmeg
1 teaspoon allspice
3 cups sifted all-purpose flour
1 teaspoon lemon rind, grated
1 teaspoon orange rind, grated
1 tablespoon lemon juice
1 egg
½ cup brown sugar, firmly packed
½ cup honey, boiling to cool
½ cup chopped candied citron (optional)
½ cup chopped nuts (optional)
candied cherries (optional, for tops)
almonds, whole, blanched (optional, for tops)

Sift and mix all dry ingredients in a large mixing bowl; stir in honey, eggs and rest of ingredients; blend well. A touch of water, perhaps, but mixture is thick and rich; chill for an hour or two.

Roll out on lightly floured board, cut into 3-by-4-inch rectangles, place on greased sheet, top with cherries and almonds. Bake in 400° F. oven for 15 minutes.

While the Lebkuchen aroma is permeating the kitchen, prepare confectioners' glaze for topping. Lebkuchen will store in cookie jar—if any is left to store!

CONFECTIONERS' SUGAR GLAZE. Blend in mixing bowl ½ teaspoon vanilla extract, ⅛ teaspoon almond extract, 1 tablespoon of cream (or milk) with a cup of sifted confectioners' sugar; stir and blend well, until it looks like a good "drizzling topping."

"Money and time are the heaviest burdens of life, and the unhappiest of all mortals are those who have more of either than they know how to use."—SAMUEL JOHNSON

Aunt Lila's Carrot Bread

My sweet sister-in-law's gastronomically admirable creation.

¾ cup salad oil
1 cup sugar
2 cups all-purpose flour (variable, or a blend of flours)
1 teaspoon baking powder
1 teaspoon cinnamon
¼ teaspoon salt
1 cup raw carrots, grated
2 eggs, beaten
½ cup nuts (your favorite), chopped
½ teaspoon vanilla

Mix all ingredients as listed and pour into well-greased loaf or tube pan. Bake in 350° F. oven for 1 hour. Glaze with your favorite topping (optional). Serve from pan, or remove and cool on rack.

"Who has lost his freedom has nothing else to lose."—German saying

Braué's Pungent Prune Wheat Bread

Fit for the proverbial monarch and entourage.

4 teaspoons baking powder
1 teaspoon salt (a bit less)
1 cup of wheat germ, blended with
1 cup of all-purpose flour
1 cup of graham flour (or your blend of rye, whole-wheat, and graham flours)
½ cup honey (or syrup or sugar)
2 tablespoons shortening (fat, oil, etc.)
1 egg, beaten
1 cup milk
1 cup cooked prunes, plus ½ cup of their juice

Blend all the dry ingredients in a mixing bowl. In another bowl, cream shortening and honey (or syrup), add egg and mix thoroughly. Combine prune juice and milk and add to creamed mixture. Add everything to the dry ingredients, plus prunes, and mix well. Bake in 350° F. oven for 1 hour.

"The object of oratory is not truth, but persuasion."—MACAULEY

Johann's Wheatless Buttermilk Rye Bread

A subtle special diet wonder for juniors and seniors—no wheat, eggs, yeast.

1 teaspoon salt
3 cups rye flour
1 teaspoon baking soda
1½ cups buttermilk
¼ cup molasses
2 tablespoons shortening, melted

½ cup seedless raisins (or figs, dates, sliced; or ¼ teaspoon each of anise and caraway seeds, or ½ teaspoon of either)
2 teaspoons baking powder

Blend flour, salt, and baking powder well. Place soda in mixing bowl with buttermilk and molasses and stir until puckery. Add flour mixture and raisins, stir well. Pour in melted shortening and stir until creamy-smooth.

Spoon into greased loaf pan (or casserole, or pot), smoothing the batter. Bake in 350° F. oven for nearly 1 hour. Cut sides of bread away from pan or pot and cool on rack, if you can!

"Make every day a cheerful day."

Braué's Hasten-mit-der-Rye Brot

Just good rye bread, quickly made. Modern living dictated this recipe.

1 tablespoon baking powder, blended with
slightly less than 1 teaspoon salt
2 cups milk
1 egg, well beaten

2 tablespoons shortening, melted
1 tablespoon orange rind, grated, or caraway seed (both optional)
3 cups rye flour

In mixing bowl, stir egg with milk. Add the shortening and baking-powder–salt mixture. Stir in the orange rind or caraway. Beat until smooth.

Spoon into greased loaf pan (or pot), bake in 325° F. oven for nearly 1 hour. Let stand in pan for a few minutes before turning loaf out to rack.

It is most gratifying to note the return to kitchen favor of the (untempered) time-tested cast-iron pot. Our Alsatian relations called it *cocotte*. Cure pots or earthenware with fat or lard.

Mother's Schleswig-Holstein Corn-Meal Bread

A most interesting and delicious recipe—prized by the youngest daughters of the Rahn-Braué families.

2¼ teaspoons baking powder
1 teaspoon salt
1 cup corn meal
1 cup whole-wheat flour
¼ cup wheat germ (preferably raw)
1 cup milk

2 tablespoons sugar, raw (or honey)
3 tablespoons shortening, melted
1 egg, beaten (mixed with milk and sugar)

In a large mixing bowl, blend the dry ingredients. Add the egg mixture, then the shortening—"und vell the shtirringk do, Phoebe, ja!"

Bake in corn-bread pan (or shallow square pan) in a 400° F. oven for nearly 30 minutes—until brown der toppen.

NOTE. Casserole, or pot, breads are usually baked uncovered, unless otherwise stated.

"Signs of progress. We need much more gear for a patio cookout than our forefathers needed to conquer the Hessians or the wilderness."

Dad's German Farmer's Graham Bread

So, so larrupin' good!

1½ teaspoons baking soda
1 teaspoon salt
¼ cup brown sugar, or maple sugar

2 cups sour milk, or butter-milk
2 cups graham flour
1 cup all-purpose flour

Blend all dry ingredients in a mixing bowl. Incorporate all other ingredients and mix well.

Turn into an oiled or greased casserole dish and bake in a 350° F. oven for 1 hour.

The following recipes are designed for persons with allergies, particularly to wheat flour.

Braué's Steamed Soybean Bread

Healthful!

1 cup soybean flour	2 cups milk or water
1 cup graham flour	3 teaspoons salt
1½ cups corn meal	1½ teaspoons baking soda
1 cup bread flour	2 cups seedless raisins
1 cup molasses	

Combine milk, salt, baking soda, and molasses. Mix well. Blend soybean flour, graham flour, corn meal, and bread flour; add to first mixture. Fold in raisins.

Place in steamer and cover with a tight lid and steam 2½ hours, or set the pan in a larger pan partly filled with water and bake in oven 1½ hours at 375° F.

"Hitch your wagon to a star."—EMERSON

Dad's Soybean Raisin-Nut Bread

A most delightful taste, and still nutritious.

2½ teaspoons baking powder	2 tablespoons sugar (or honey)
¼ teaspoon salt	1 tablespoon melted shortening (or oil)
2 cups sifted white flour	⅔ cup seedless raisins
1 cup soybean flour	½ cup chopped nuts (optional)
1 egg, fairly beaten	
1 cup milk	

Blend the dry ingredients together in a large bowl. In another bowl mix milk, egg, sugar, and shortening; add to flour mixture, stirring until smooth. Add raisins and nuts. Mix until there is no question of the smooth texture.

Spoon into greased loaf pan, and bake in 345° F. oven for nearly 1 hour.

"Time and opportunity are no man's slave." Deutsche saying

Braué's Soybean Spoon Bread

Yankee version.

½ teaspoon baking soda
¼ teaspoon salt
1 cup soybean flour
1 egg, beaten

1 cup buttermilk
1 tablespoon melted shortening

Beat flour, soda, and salt in large mixing bowl. In another bowl combine egg, shortening, and buttermilk; add to flour mixture, stirring well.

Spoon into well-greased pan, bake at 350° F. for 1 hour, and serve while hot, with butter!

"A wager is a fool's argument."

Braué's Southern Soybean Spoon Bread

The South rises again, suh, to a golden, tasty brown.

2 teaspoons baking powder
⅓ cup soybean flour
⅓ cup corn meal
1 teaspoon salt
1 tablespoon sugar (or honey)

2 cups milk, scalded
2 tablespoons melted butter
(or oil)
3 eggs, unbeaten

Combine soybean flour, corn meal, and salt in a deep pan; pour in milk, stirring the while. Cook over slow fire, still stirring, until smooth and thick. Add melted butter and sugar, stirring, then remove from heat. Add eggs, blending well and "Confederately"; add baking powder, beating well.

Pour batter into greased deep pie pan or shallow casserole and bake in a 410° F. oven for 30 minutes. Serve hot with butter, and let's hear that ole rebel yell!

"Youth—by dates? Nay, by deeds!"

Phoebe's Extra-special Soybean Corn Bread

This might take the place of your family recipe for corn bread.

2 cups corn meal
¼ cup soybean flour
1 cup all-purpose flour
1 teaspoon baking powder
½ teaspoon baking soda (in a small portion of hot water)
½ teaspoon salt

¼ cup granulated sugar
1 egg, beaten
3 tablespoons melted shortening
Sour milk (enough to make a soft mixture)

Blend the flours, baking powder, and salt with the corn meal. Add the egg, sugar, and shortening; stir sour milk into the soda mixture, then mix with the flour mixture, stirring all to a soft mix.

Spoon into a well-greased pan. Bake in a 400° F. oven for 30 minutes.

"Better keep peace than make peace."—Dutch proverb

There is no other taste sensation to equal the heavenly bite of a home-baked treat right from your own oven. If you are more than forty years young, you will remember with keen nostalgia the aroma of yeast breads baking in someone's homey kitchen!

"Some folks are wise, some are otherwise."—SMOLLETT

Now is an excellent time for two versions of corn bread, *richtig?* I will present the Yankee Corn Bread recipe first, to be polite, for I married a delightful west Texas gal!

Braué's Yankee Corn Bread

1 cup white or yellow corn meal
½ teaspoon salt
2 tablespoons melted shortening

1 cup milk
1 egg
1 tablespoon sugar
1 cup white flour
1½ teaspoons baking powder

Beat the egg well in a large bowl and add the moist ingredients. Mix and remix the dry ingredients in another bowl, then combine with egg mixture, constantly stirring. Mix thoroughly, and you will be delighted with the baked result.

Pour into greased baking pan or muffin pan and bake in 350° F. oven for less than 30 minutes. Rebels, you all will take to this mix, too!

Braué's Golden Southern Corn Bread

1 cup yellow corn meal
1 teaspoon salt
¼ cup melted shortening
1 cup milk

2 eggs
2 tablespoons sugar
1 cup flour
3 teaspoons baking powder

Beat eggs well in a large bowl, then add milk and shortening. Mix dry ingredients in another large bowl; then add to egg mixture, stirring well until moist. Pour into greased square pan or cornstick pans, and bake in 400° F. oven for nearly 25 minutes. Mighty good, pahdnahs!

Mother followed this recipe, seconded by Earlene, except for a bit more corn meal, milk, sugar, and baking powder in relation to the eggs.

Dad's German Farmer's Sour-Cream Bread

A most hospitable bread for all.

6 eggs, beaten
3 tablespoons oil (preheated in large casserole dish in oven)
2 teaspoons salt
¼ cup nutritional brewers' yeast (or wheat germ)
1 quart sour cream
4 cups corn meal (white or yellow); also delicious with some flour blends

Blend and incorporate well into the casserole dish all ingredients after the oil has been heated slightly. (This mixture may be divided equally into smaller casserole dishes or pie pans.) Bake at 350° F. for 40 minutes. Cut into wedges for serving.

Dad's Boston Brown Bread

What a hit with the men! Superior with Boston baked beans and Old Country butter. If you are able to find an old Boston brown-bread pan with the lid on it, you are in luck!

½ teaspoon salt
½ teaspoon baking soda
¼ cup sugar
1 tablespoon melted butter or margarine
2 cups all-purpose flour
1 cup whole-wheat or graham flour

1 egg, beaten
¼ cup molasses
¾ cup sour milk
¼ cup chopped walnuts
¼ cup raisins
(These last two items may be left out entirely, for old-timers' sakes!)

Beat egg thoroughly in large bowl. Add molasses, butter, and sugar, stirring the while.

Blend the flours; then add to egg mixture, along with salt, soda, and sour milk. Beat thoroughly (add nuts and raisins, if desired) and mix well.

This is a real good time to use a one-pound coffee can, greased well. Fill can half full, cover tightly, and place in your pressure saucepan. Add about 3 cups of boiling water, cover saucepan, and for 15 to 20 minutes steam without pressure, then for 40 minutes at 15 pounds of pressure. Remove from pan and from can, and eat or cool. If it isn't gone at the first sitting, use coffee can for storing.

"A wise man knows everything, a shrewd one everybody."

Boston Brown Bread (Midwestern)

Another of Dad's tasty versions of this wonderful bread!

1 egg
1 cup sour milk
¼ cup molasses
½ teaspoon salt
½ teaspoon soda

1 cup yellow corn meal
1 cup white flour
1 teaspoon baking powder
1 cup whole-wheat or graham flour

Beat egg well in large bowl, then add all the moist ingredients, stirring the while. Add all the dry ingredients. Beat and blend well.

Place in well-greased round brown-bread cans, coffee cans, or deep baking dishes. Cover, and place in a shallow pan with more than a film of water. Bake in a 350° F. oven for 90 minutes.

"Words without thoughts never to heaven go."—SHAKESPEARE

Mrs. Hammill's Johnnycake Bread

This cake was made especially for young Johann by gracious neighbors, the Hammills, who owned and managed the Hammill Business College in Council Bluffs, Iowa. While we nibbled at this tasty titbit in our music class at Washington Avenue School, our enthusiastic teacher would lead us in the lilting song "Oh, No, John, No, John, No, John, No!"

1 egg	¾ cup brown sugar (packed
½ teaspoon baking soda	firmly)
½ teaspoon salt	½ cup buttermilk (or sour
1 cup yellow corn meal	milk)
1 cup all purpose flour (or unbleached)	½ cup sour cream

Beat egg thoroughly in large bowl, then add all liquid ingredients, stirring as you add. Blend and mix; set aside while you blend and mix all dry ingredients together in another bowl. Make a small well in the dry ingredients and pour the egg mixture into the "dry" bowl, slowly does it, stirring the while. Beat until the first full smoothness appears, then turn mix into greased cookie pan. Bake in a 430° F. oven 18 minutes or until the broom straw "from center comes out spick-and-span." Johnnycake is satisfyingly delicious hot, with butter and maple syrup!

Someone said, "A ragged colt may make a good horse." Sounds like our boy, young Jeb the Reb.

"Wit is the salt of conversation, not the food."—HAZLITT

Earlene's Banana-Nut Bread

Mein Frau's prize recipe.

4 cups flour	⅔ cup shortening
4 teaspoons baking powder	1⅓ cups sugar
½ teaspoon baking soda	4 eggs, beaten
1 teaspoon salt	3 cups mashed banana

1 cup chopped pecans, if desired

Sift together dry ingredients. Cream shortening and sugar, add eggs, and beat thoroughly. Alternate dry mixture, and mashed bananas and nuts, into egg mixture. Final mix will be quite stiff, unless the bananas you use are very ripe. Place in two greased loaf pans and bake 1 hour 10 minutes at 350° F.

This bread gets better, better, and better. It is especially good sliced, buttered, and toasted, but is so good by itself that you may not get a chance to toast it! A loaf makes a most welcome holiday gift.

"The fool rages and is confident."—The Bible

Dad's Bran Banana-Nut Bread

Guaranteed to make you famous as a kaffee klatch hostess, along with kaffee kuchen, of course.

½ teaspoon salt	¼ cup shortening
2 teaspoons baking powder	1 egg
½ teaspoon soda	1 cup bran (cereal or flour
1 teaspoon vanilla extract	bran)
½ cup sugar	2 tablespoons water
½ cup chopped nuts (optional)	2 cups ripe bananas
3 cups flour, all-purpose	

Beat egg well in large bowl; mash bananas in another bowl. Mix shortening and sugar with egg, then stir bran, bananas, and water into mixture. Mix well; then add the rest of sifted dry ingredients, stirring constantly. Add vanilla (and nuts if wished), and mix until creamy smooth. Bake in a greased loaf pan at 345° F. for 60 minutes.

Phoebe's Deutsche Kaffee Kuchen

This is one of the most delectable of coffee cakes, and we are sure you possess a variation of the following, baked many happy times by your mothers and grandmothers.

¼ teaspoon salt
1 cup sugar (or honey)
¼ cup shortening
1 teaspoon baking powder
2 egg yolks, beaten
2 egg whites, beaten to stiffness
½ cup milk
2 cups flour, all-purpose

Topping:
¼ cup brown sugar
6 tablespoons flour
2 tablespoons butter
½ teaspoon baking powder

In large bowl thoroughly mix sugar, egg yolks, and shortening until creamy. Stir in flour, baking powder, salt, and milk; then fold in egg whites. Mix until smooth.

Pour into greased or wax-paper-lined round or square (8-inch) pan. Blend (with fork, 'tis good) the topping ingredients and sprinkle over top of der kuchen mixen. Bake in 350° F. oven for 45 pre-kaffee-klatsch minutes. Serve in wedges or squares.

Dad's Raisin-Bran Quick Brown Bread

Quickly baked, quickly gone!

3 teaspoons baking powder
½ cup sugar
2 cups all-purpose flour
¼ teaspoon salt
½ cup seedless raisins
1 cup milk

3 tablespoons molasses
1 cup whole bran (or cereal)
1 egg, well beaten
4 tablespoons melted butter or shortening

Stir and blend all dry ingredients except bran in large bowl; add raisins and stir. In another bowl, place bran. Pour milk and molasses over bran, stirring constantly; then add egg and shortening, stirring. Add this mixture to flour mixture and blend well; mix until rich and smooth-appearing.

Spoon into loaf or casserole dish (greased) and bake in 350° F. oven for 60 minutes.

Mother's Banana-Date Bread

My mother used to bake this for her girl friends, holidays, week ends and talk-time.

1 cup bananas, thoroughly mashed (3 bananas)
1 tablespoon lemon juice (squeezed or bottled)
½ cup shortening (butter, margarine, oil, or lard)
½ cup sugar (variable), creamed with the shortening
1 teaspoon soda, blended with salt and flour, stirred well
½ teaspoon salt
1 cup dates, pitted and chopped
1 cup nuts (your favorites) chopped
3 cups all-purpose flour (variable—soy, unbleached; Mother blended a "touch bit" of rye with the white flour)

Mix the lemon juice and bananas well and add the creamed sugar and shortening, all in a large mixing bowl. Add the blended flour, salt, and soda mixture plus the dates and nuts and stir well, until creamy-moist.

Spoon into loaf pan (or casserole: Mother used a cast-iron pan), well greased, and bake in 350° F. oven for an hour. Scrumptious with butter and spiced tea!

Yes, friends, Texas is different: it appeals to the young and young at heart, for it still presents a pioneering spirit, a sense of belonging, an exuberant individualism plus friendliness, variety of living (even weather—we in west Texas can watch the four seasons go by in one day), vastness and freedom of the Tejas poem: .

> The sun has riz,
> The sun has set,
> And here we is
> In Texas yet!

"Things won are done; joy's soul lies in the doing."
—SHAKESPEARE

Braué's Old-fashioned Jewish Honey Cake

A holiday treat—zestful—bar mizvahs!

1 teaspoon baking powder
1 teaspoon baking soda
1 teaspoon cinnamon
1 cup very strong black coffee
(Louisiana style)
1 teaspoon allspice
2 eggs, beaten

¾ cup honey
1 cup sugar
½ cup salad oil
3 cups all-purpose flour, sifted
½ cup nuts, not chopped too
fine (optional)

In a large mixing bowl, add oil to eggs, stirring. Add honey and coffee; then add sugar, gradually, plus all dry ingredients (sifted together), mixing thoroughly until a colorful smoothness.

Pour into a greased loaf pan and bake in a 325° F. oven for an hour.

"The sting of reproach is the truth of it."

Braué's Passover Rolls

1 cup boiling water in saucepan
½ cup oil
1 tablespoon sugar

1 teaspoon salt
2 cups matzo meal
4 eggs, beaten

Add oil to boiling water, keeping saucepan over low heat. Add sugar, salt, and matzo meal, beating rapidly until mixture forms a ball. Remove from heat and beat in eggs, slowly; then beat vigorously until batter is smooth-thick.

Shape into balls and place on greased cookie sheet; with a sharp knife, slash a design on top of each ball. Bake in 370° F. oven for an hour.

"Time is the best adviser."—PERICLES

Johann's Old-fashioned Peach Kuchen Brot

A pleasant memory of Sunday with Grossmutter, Tante Carrie, and our Uncle Johann

4 teaspoons baking powder
¾ teaspoon salt
¼ teaspoon mace
½ cup sugar
1 cup milk
1 egg, beaten well
½ stick of butter melted (or oil, margarine)

3 cups all-purpose flour (or a blend of flours)

Topping:
2 cups peaches, thinly sliced
1 teaspoon cinnamon
2 tablespoons sugar
sour cream

Blend the dry ingredients in a large mixing bowl. In another bowl combine egg, butter, and milk. Spoon into the dry ingredients and beat until fully blended.

Spoon the batter into a greased casserole dish and cover top of batter with 2 cups of thinly sliced peaches (fresh, frozen, or canned). Sprinkle the peaches with a blend of cinnamon and sugar and bake in a 375° F. oven for at least 35 minutes.

Remove from the oven and spread sour cream evenly over the top of the kuchen. Return to the oven for at least 5 minutes.

The peach kuchen may be placed in the refrigerator for several days. Just heat in the oven to serve.

"Genius rusts for want of use."

Sons of Erin Soda Bread

Father Callahan's favorite . . . History would have been much different if Irish-Deutsche diplomacy had been as rich and wholesome as their legendary hearty baking. This recipe has smoothed many a ruffled "red-neck" und "stiff-neck."

1 tablespoon soda
1 tablespoon sugar
4 cups all-purpose flour (unbleached flour and white flours)

2½ teaspoons salt
¼ teaspoon cream of tartar
2 cups buttermilk
1 tablespoon butter ("the size of an egg")

Combine soda, flour, sugar, salt, and cream of tartar in large mixing bowl; mix thoroughly. Add buttermilk, and with mixing fork stir this mixture until moist.

Turn out onto a lightly floured board and knead through one verse of "Mother Machree." Shape into a ball, place on a greased cookie sheet, flatten a bit, then, with a sharp knife, slash the bloomin' top fourrrr times.

Bake in a 375° F. oven for nearly 45 minutes. Remove to wire rack, brush the top with butter, then cool.

Now, sons, for St. Patrick's Day, combine a bit over a cup of raisins and some caraway seeds with the dry ingredients above, or some nuts and fruit, if you wish.

"Rags are royal raiment when worn for virtue's sake."

—CAMPBELL

St. Patrick's Day Oatmeal Bread

A real all-nation special, "with the wearin' o' the green" this has solved many misunderstandings.

1½ tablespoons baking powder
1¼ cups quick rolled oats
3 cups all-purpose flour (unbleached flour and white flours)
1 tablespoon salt

¼ cup honey
1 cup milk (variable)
1 egg, from der farm commen
1 tablespoon butter or margarine (or oil)

An excellent spot for herb experimenting, sparingly, at first— the soup herbs.

Mix all the dry ingredients in a large bowl. In another bowl beat the honey, milk, and egg. Pour egg mixture into flour mixture, stir with wooden spoon until mixture is moist.

Spoon mixture into large greased bread pan and bake in 350° F. oven for 70 gremlin minutes; the top will be crusty brown. Turn loaf out on wire rack, and brush top with butter. Leprechaunish lusciousness!

"By the work we know the workman."—LA FONTAINE

Dad's Kilarney, Emerald Isle, St. Patrick's Bread
A March 17 favorite of all.

4 teaspoons baking powder
1 teaspoon salt
2 teaspoons cinnamon
½ cup sugar
4 cups all-purpose flour (or a blend of flours)
2 cups milk

1 egg, beaten
3 tablespoons orange peel, grated
1 cup currants (or seedless raisins)
2 tablespoons shortening, melted (or nutritional oils)

Blend all dry ingredients in large mixing bowl. Mix remaining ingredients in another bowl. Spoon a well in dry ingredients and add the shortening mixture, beating until smooth. For further wearin' o' the green, drop a few dashes of green coloring into the mix.

Spoon batter into oiled or greased casserole dish, let stand for a few moments while you make sure der goot oven has been preheated to 350° F. Bake for at least 50 minutes. Cut and serve in wedges, or remove to cool on rack. Can be stored in refrigerator in moisture/vapor-proof paper.

"It is often better not to see an insult than to avenge it."—SENECA

MUFFINS

Muffins are true quick blends. Blend the dry ingredients thoroughly and make a well in center. Cool shortening a bit, then stir all liquid ingredients together. Add to dry ingredients until all is moist; batter will be lumpy. Drop batter into lightly greased muffin-pan cups (two-thirds full), and bake in moderate to hot oven until crust is a "harvest-brown." Crust will steam if left in pans. Variations are endless (fruits, nuts, jams, jellies).

Mother's Mellow Muffins
A basic recipe for many variations.

3 teaspoons baking powder
½ teaspoon salt
¼ cup sugar (or honey)
2 cups flour

¼ cup shortening, melted
1 egg, beaten
1 cup milk

Blend dry ingredients. In another bowl, combine liquid ingredients, then add them to dry ingredients, stirring until moist. This recipe will fill 12 greased muffin cups. Bake in 400° F. oven for 20 to 25 minutes.

JELLY MUFFINS. Top batter with 1 teaspoon of favorite jelly before baking.

WHEAT-GERM MUFFINS. Add ½ cup wheat germ to dry ingredients.

CORN MUFFINS. Add 1 cup milk and 1 cup corn meal.

BRAN MUFFINS. Add 1 cup bran; reduce flour a bit.

SOUR-MILK MUFFINS. Substitute sour milk for sweet milk; reduce baking powder to 2 teaspoons and add about 1 teaspoon soda.

NUT, RAISIN or DATE MUFFINS. Add ½ cup of nuts, raisins or chopped dates, and stir into batter quickly.

BLUEBERRY MUFFINS. Add ½ cup of blueberries and reduce milk to ½ cup.

"Knowledge comes, but history lingers."—TENNYSON

Mother's Whole-Wheat Muffins

¼ cup shortening
¼ cup sugar
2 eggs
3 teaspoons baking powder
½ teaspoon salt

3 cups whole-wheat and graham flour (mixed to your satisfaction, with white or soy flours, also)
2 cups milk

Cream together shortening and sugar; add eggs and beat well. Blend flour, baking powder, and salt; add alternately with the milk to creamed mixture, stirring only enough to dampen flour. Fill well-greased muffin pans two-thirds full. ("Hans, der pans full, nodt qvidte.")

Bake in hot oven (425° F.) 20 to 25 minutes. Makes 12 large muffins. A taste feast with butter, jam, and milk or coffee!

Whole-wheat dough ferments much faster than does white dough, so please keep your whole-wheat dough soft!

"A hasty man never wants woe."

Dad's Soybean-Flour Muffins

1 teaspoon baking powder
½ teaspoon salt
1 cup soybean flour
⅓ cup milk (can be nonfat)

1 tablespoon melted shortening (or oil)
1 egg beaten

Sift dry ingredients together in a large bowl. In another bowl blend milk, shortening, egg. Then stir this mixture swiftly into the dry ingredients; blend lightly but well.

Spoon into greased muffin pan, and bake in 425° F. oven for 15 minutes.

"Whoever lives true life will love true love."—BROWNING

Braué Home Bakery Diabetic Health Muffins

**Recommended by physicians and dieticians, particularly my parents'
dear friends, Drs. Mary and Matt.**

1½ teaspoons baking powder
pinch of salt
¼ cup soybean flour
⅛ cup gluten flour

¼ cup whole-wheat flour
1 egg, well beaten
1¼ tablespoons melted butter
1 cup milk (variable)

Sift together all the flours, blend well; mix all dry ingredients
with flours. Then add the egg, slowly stirring in the milk too,
plus the butter, for a stiff batter.

Spoon into well-greased muffin tins. Bake in 375° F. oven for
30 minutes.

Persons not on a diabetic diet may add ¼ cup sugar to this
recipe.

"Stop eating when you are enjoying it most."—Deutsche saying
by a very Lean Dutchman (or one whose wife nagged, I'm sure!)

BISCUITS

Biscuits, the delectable delight of all, have a resultant goodness if prepared thus: Blend all dry ingredients, cut in shortening with pastry blender until crumbly. Make a well in center of coarse mixture, add all liquids, stir until the dough tags after the spoon or fork.

Turn out on lightly floured surface, knead (oh, most gently) for a slow count a bit less than your age—gentle handling produces flakier biscuits. Pat, or roll, dough out evenly (first-knuckle-point-of-thumb thickness), cut with floured biscuit cutter. Place on ungreased baking sheet and bake in 450° F. oven for 15 minutes (variable).

For crusty drop biscuits, add a bit more liquid.

Blend all dry ingredients the night before, plus cutting in the shortening, and store in refrigerator.

Phoebe's Soybean-Flour Baking-Powder Biscuits
The greatest!

2 teaspoons baking powder
1 cup all-purpose flour
¼ cup soybean flour

½ teaspoon salt
2 tablespoons shortening
½ cup milk

First sift the flours well, then the baking powder and salt, in a large bowl. Cut in the shortening; add the milk and mix well.

Roll out on a lightly floured board; but do not handle too much as you knead. Roll out dough ½ inch thick.

Cut into biscuits, place on greased cookie sheet, bake in 450° F. oven for 15 minutes. Has a delightful rich flavor with bonus protein value.

"Make not your sauce until you've caught your fish."—ANON.

Mother's Home Biscuits

Memorable moments of most homes.

3 teaspoons baking powder	4 tablespoons shortening
½ teaspoon salt	1 cup milk
2 cups flour	

Blend all dry ingredients, cut in shortening until crumbly-coarse. Add milk and stir until dough follows stirring.

Turn out onto lightly floured surface, knead gently for 30 seconds. Roll out, cut into desired size, and bake on ungreased baking sheets in 450° F. oven for 15 minutes (varies as to altitude).

BUTTERMILK BISCUITS. Substitute buttermilk for milk, add ¼ teaspoon soda.

TEA BISCUITS. Add 2 teaspoons sugar and ¼ teaspoon cream of tartar.

WHOLE-WHEAT BISCUITS. Substitute whole-wheat flour for white flour.

SOUR-DOUGH BISCUITS. Use 1 cup sour-dough starter with milk and a bit of flour the night before. In the morning, mix as usual, but add dash of baking soda.

Johann's Old-fashioned Sweet-Potato Biscuits

Remember, Grandmother?

1 cup sweet potatoes (mashed or puréed)	1 tablespoon sugar (or honey)
1 cup milk (or stock)	½ teaspoon salt
4 tablespoons butter	2 cups all-purpose flour (or a blend of unbleached white and dark flours)
4 teaspoons baking powder	

Blend and mix well all ingredients until delightfully smooth. Turn out on a lightly floured board. Roll out into a ½-inch-thick sheet. Cut with cookie cutters. Place on greased cookie pans. Bake in a 450° F. oven for 15 minutes.

Uncle John's Sour-Cream Biscuits

Be prepared to bake many of these gems, Mother.

1 tablespoon baking powder	1 cup dairy sour cream
¼ teaspoon baking soda	¼ cup milk
1 teaspoon salt	a bit of melted butter (oil or
2 cups all-purpose flour	margarine)

Blend all dry ingredients. Add and blend sour cream. Stir in the milk and stir well to make a soft dough.

Turn onto a lightly floured board and knead gently. Roll with a rolling pin, or pat to a thickness of ½ or ¾ inch. Cut with biscuit cutter. Place on a lightly greased or oiled baking sheet.

Bake in a 450° F. preheated oven for 10 minutes. Brush the tops with melted butter. Serve immediately.

"Nothing is well said or done in passion."

DOUGHNUTS

Doughnuts, fine family fare, are freshly fashioned from soft dough and easily handled. They should rest a bit after being cut with a floured doughnut cutter.

Turn only once (with a long wooden stick) as you fry der little crullers in hot deep fat (around 375° F., but no hotter).

Drain on soft flour sacking, tea towels, or absorbent paper. Dust doughnuts with sugar in paper sack.

Dad's Famous Raised Sugar Doughnuts

"Melt-in-your-mouth depression dainties" that sold for fifteen cents a dozen.

1 package of active dry yeast, dissolved in
1 cup water, warm
1 cup milk, scalded to luke- warm
8 cups flour (variable)

½ cup shortening
1 cup sugar (or honey, or brown sugar)
½ teaspoon salt
2 eggs, beaten

Add milk to yeast water. Add half of the flour and beat until satiny-smooth. Cover and let stand in a warm place for a morning or afternoon. Thoroughly cream the remaining ingredients, except for the rest of flour. Beat well, thoroughly incorporate everything, including the balance of the flour. Turn out on lightly floured board, knead lightly, cover and let rise overnight.

Next morning knead; then let rise until doubled in bulk. Roll out, cut with doughnut cutters, and fry in deep fat at 375° F., until brown. Drain and dust with sugar, or sugar and cinnamon.

"A wise traveler never despises his own country."—GOLDINI

Raised Doughnut Dough Variations

DAD'S BAVARIAN BISMARCKS. Using cooky cutter, cut out round shapes. Place a generous jibble of jelly or preserves in center of each round; fold each one and seal edges like a purse. Fry, drain, dust, or top with frosting.

SPICED DOUGHNUTS. Add ¼ teaspoon each of nutmeg, cinnamon, ginger, and mace to the dry ingredients.

MOLASSES DOUGHNUTS. Add a cup of molasses and omit 1 egg.

"A merry heart maketh a cheerful countenance."—The Bible

Dad's Cake Doughnuts

Full-flavored quickies for the teen-age set.

4 teaspoons baking powder
1 teaspoon salt
1 teaspoon cinnamon
½ teaspoon nutmeg
4 cups flour

2 tablespoons shortening
1 cup sugar
2 eggs, beaten
1 cup milk

Blend all dry ingredients well. Cream shortening and sugar, add eggs, beat well. Add milk and dry ingredients, thoroughly incorporating. Roll out on lightly floured board, cut with floured doughnut cutter. Rest doughnuts for a spell.

Fry in deep fat at 375° F. until brown. Drain and devour.

"Three may keep counsel, if two be away."—HEYWOOD

Tante Carrie's Crullers

Toothsome kaffee klatsch tasties!

2 tablespoons shortening, melted
1 cup sugar
1 cup milk or cream
3 eggs, beaten

3 tablespoons baking powder
½ teaspoon salt
4 cups flour (all-purpose or blend)
½ teaspoon nutmeg

Combine dry ingredients, except sugar, blending well. Cream shortening and sugar, add eggs and beat well. Add milk (or cream) and dry ingredients; mix thoroughly. Chill if you wish.

Roll out on floured surface. Cut into strips and knot or twist and seal them. Fry in 365° F. deep fat. Drain and dust with powdered or granulated sugar.

"A beaten path is a safe one."—Latin proverb

Mother's Apple Fritters

Ambrosial memories!

2 teaspoons baking powder	1 cup milk
2 dashes of salt	1 egg, beaten
2 tablespoons sugar	crab or tarty apples, pared and
2 cups all-purpose flour (variable)	sliced

Blend all dry ingredients. Add milk and egg and incorporate thoroughly. Dip apple slices in batter for complete coating and fry in 370° F. deep fat for 3 minutes. Serve with syrups or jellies.

"The best prophet of the future is the past."—BYRON

GRIDDLE CAKES

Griddle cakes, containing very few ingredients, are easy to make (or so say the boys on a campout). Stir batter till all is moist, then stop.

The griddle does not need to be greased if 2 or more tablespoons of shortening are used for each cup of liquid of der batch innen. The griddle is ready when drops of water jump on surface.

Drop batter with pitcher and spoon (or just spoon), and cook until top is bubbly; "turn vunce," but only.

Pancakes make happy people and are baked on griddles all over the world.

Try all flours, for goodness' sake, fellows, for real fluffy Pfannkuchen. On der campout yedt, save the milk for the children und in der batter beer geputten!

"Envy shoots at others and wounds itself."

Mother's Pancakes

Basic gusty recipe of the Rahns . . . ideal spot for the sour-dough starter.

1 tablespoon baking powder	1 egg, beaten
½ teaspoon salt	1 cup milk
a bit of sugar (or honey)	3 tablespoons butter, melted
3 cups flour	(oil, etc.)

Blend dry ingredients thoroughly. In another bowl, combine rest of ingredients. Add to dry ingredients; stir until all is just moist—batter may be lumpy.

Bake on ungreased griddle.

VARIATIONS. Add ½ cup of fruit to batter (berries, apples, pineapple, jellies) and serve flat or rolled with butter, powdered sugar, honey, and syrup.

SOUR-MILK VARIATION. Reduce amount of baking powder a bit and add ½ teaspoon of soda. Substitute sour milk for milk.

"Zeal without knowledge is fire without light."—FULLER

Mother's Alsatian Pancakes

A piquant and provocative blend from positive parents.

¼ teaspoon salt
1 cup potatoes, mashed
1 cup flour
4 egg yolks, beaten

2 cups potato water and milk (any type of milk, even evaporated)
4 egg whites, stiffly beaten

Completely combine all ingredients, folding in egg whites last. Stir until moist and bake on ungreased griddle. Serve with your favorite topping.

"He who talks much is sometimes right."—Spanish proverb

Dad's Pronto Country Buckwheat Cakes

Relishingly savory pioneers.

4 teaspoons baking powder
1 teaspoon salt
1 tablespoon sugar or honey (optional)
1 cup buckwheat flour
1 cup white flour

1 egg, beaten
2 cups milk (if sour milk, reduce baking powder to 3 teaspoons and add 1 teaspoon soda)
½ cup shortening, melted

Blend all of the dry ingredients well the night before. Add the rest of ingredients, and stir until smooth and moist. Bake on ungreased griddle. Goes well with all toppings.

"He who loses his temper is in the wrong."—French proverb

Dad's Own Sour-Dough Pancakes

For those who cannot claim a starter that goes back to Grandmother or Grandfather.

Starter:

1 cake yeast	2 cups warm water
2 cups flour	(or please try a basic starter)

Dissolve yeast in warm water and add flour; stir, then set in a warm place overnight. In morning, take out ½ cup of mixture, pour in a scalded jar, cover, and store in refrigerator. This is your starter for future breakfasts. Now, to the mix left in bowl, add—stirringly!—

1 teaspoon baking soda	2 tablespoons shortening,
½ teaspoon salt	melted
1 egg, beaten	1 tablespoon sugar

Mix well; add a little milk if batter is too thick. Cook on hot griddle. Do not add leftover batter to starter, but if there is any batter left over (I cannot believe it!), serve it as muffins or pancakes later on, with fresh berries!

"You will have a better chance of leaving your footsteps on the sands of time if you wear work shoes."—JOHN C. VIVIAN

Mother's Alsatian Pfannkuchen

Crepes!

3 eggs, beaten	2 tablespoons oil
pinch of salt	2 cups flour
2 cups of milk	butter for cooking

Mix all ingredients until consistency of heavy cream. Sizzle butter in 6-inch skillet and pour in batter to just cover bottom, rotating skillet as batter is poured. Cook until tender brown. Stack if they are to be filled with jellies, or fold and roll if to be served with sauces.

"A little fact is worth a whole limbo of dreams."—EMERSON

Dad's Soybean Quick Mix

A quick mix with variations; the basic dry mix consists of:

½ lb. flour (blended 2 to 1, white or dark flours to soybean)
1½ ounces baking powder
pinch salt

2½ ounces shortening (more for pancakes and waffles)
1 egg (2 eggs for pancake mix)
milk to make biscuit batter (more milk for pancake mix)

Work and experimentation with this quick mix resulted in Dad's pioneering recipes of goodness for diabetics.

Dad's Quick Soybean Pancake-Waffle Mix

This healthful prize was shipped all over the country by railroad and streetcar men until my talented parents' deaths before World War II.

2½ lbs. wheat flour (or rice and/or corn flours)
1¼ lbs. soybean flour
2½ ounces baking powder
¾ ounce salt

1¾ ounces sugar (optional; out, of course, in diabetic mix)
¼ lb. nonfat dry milk

These mixes show that the need for eggs and milk is greatly reduced.

Dad's Deutsche Kartoffel-Pfannkuchen

(*German Potato Pancakes*)

Groombeer—gemutlichkeit! A mainstay of so many Deutsche families of the old country.

3 potatoes, grated into cold water
1 onion, grated
½ teaspoon salt
1 egg, beaten

½ cup flour
2 tablespoons sour milk
1 cup cooking oil, heated very hot in skillet

Drain potatoes, beat in the rest of ingredients, and drop mixture into skillet. Fry on both sides until brown.

WAFFLES

Waffles are made up of rich-flavored, smooth, thin batters that may be stored for a brief time in the refrigerator. Shortening should be cooled before adding to the batter, and eggs folded in last. Do not grease waffle iron—you will get long-baking, crisper, crunchier "squares"! Shortcake batters make rich-flavored waffles, but must be baked over low heat. Waffles are done when steam stops coming from waffle iron; do not raise cover while batter is baking. Never let egg yolks tarry with whites when beating separately, as yolks contain fat.

Mother's Fluffy Waffles

Early in the morning, or in "the shank of the evening."

3 teaspoons baking powder
½ teaspoon salt
2 cups flour (all-purpose or a blend of soy and wheat flours variable)

2 egg yolks, beaten
2 cups milk
1 cup shortening, melted
2 eggs whites, beaten

Blend dry ingredients. Combine egg yolks, milk, and melted fat and stir into dry ingredients. Fold in egg whites. Fill waffle iron and bake until steam no longer appears.

BACON WAFFLES. Sprinkle finely-cut-up bacon over batter after poured on iron.

HAM WAFFLES. Add finely chopped ham to batter before folding in egg whites.

APPLE WAFFLES. Add a cup of chopped apples, a tablespoon of blended cinnamon, and sugar to batter before folding in egg white.

NUT WAFFLES. Add a cup of crushed nuts to batter before folding in egg white.

SOUTHERN BUTTERMILK WAFFLES. Use only 1 egg and substitute buttermilk for milk.

Yeast and Specialty Breads

"The greater the difficulty, the more glory in surmounting it."
—Epicurus

WHEAT AND BLENDED-FLOUR BREADS

In these tense days, abnormality appears to be normal, and modern bread is no exception. By contrast, the following recipes that are marked with an asterisk (*) are delicious and health-giving. Interestingly enough, these recipes were given to Dad by descendants of the Mormons who settled in the area after the Saints had crossed the river at Kanesville (Council Bluffs, Iowa). And, strangely enough, these same recipes are followed religiously in several Catholic monasteries. Both churches attest to the fact that these recipes, properly followed, are wholly responsible for the magnificent health of the persons involved, whose daily diet is somewhat restricted.

"Order is Heaven's first law."—Pope

Braué's Whole-Wheat Bread*

1 cake fresh active yeast (or 1 pkg. dry yeast)
½ cup lukewarm water
1 tablespoon shortening
1 tablespoon honey
1 tablespoon molasses
1 tablespoon salt
3 cups scalded milk
6 cups whole-wheat flour

Soften yeast in water. Melt shortening and combine with honey, molasses, salt, and scalded milk. Cool to lukewarm and combine with the yeast mixture. Add the flour, enough to make a soft dough, and knead thoroughly, using extra flour when needed. Place in bowl and cover with clean tea towel; let rise in warm area, away from drafts, until slightly less than double in bulk. Punch down and shape into two loaf pans. Let rise to "not quite" double in bulk and bake at 350° F. for sixty minutes.

Braué's All Saints' Graham Bread*

2 cups starter, or
1 cup compressed yeast
¼ cup lukewarm water
2 tablespoons sugar (or honey)
2 cups milk, scalded

1 tablespoon salt
6 cups whole-wheat or graham flour
2 tablespoons softened shortening
3 cups sifted all-purpose flour

Crumble yeast into lukewarm water; add 1 teaspoon sugar. Stir well, let stand in warm place until foamy. Pour milk into mixing bowl; add remaining sugar and salt. Cool until lukewarm; add yeast. Add 3 cups whole-wheat flour; beat thoroughly. Add shortening, stir in enough all-purpose flour to make a soft dough. Let dough stand 10 minutes.

Turn out on floured board; knead 10 minutes, working in all remaining flour, until dough is soft but not sticky. Shape into ball; place in greased bowl. Brush with shortening, cover with towel, and let rise in warm place (80°–85° F.), free from drafts, until double in bulk.

Shape dough into two loaves; place in greased pans. Brush with shortening, cover; let rise until double, as before. Bake in hot oven (400° F.) 10 minutes, then reduce to moderately hot (375° F.) and bake 30 to 40 minutes longer.

"Discretion in speech is more than eloquence."

Braué's Whole-Wheat Rolls*

Do you remember this, hot out of the oven with fresh milk?

1 cake yeast (compressed or dry)
1 cup lukewarm water
6 tablespoons melted shortening

5 tablespoons sugar (brown or granulated)
1 tablespoon salt
1 cup milk, scalded
6 cups whole-wheat flour

Dissolve yeast in lukewarm water. Dissolve shortening, sugar, and salt in scalded milk; cool to lukewarm. Mix together yeast and milk mixtures. Stir in enough flour, mixing well to form soft dough. Knead on lightly floured board until smooth and satiny (as you did with the bread mix).

Shape dough into ball; place in greased bowl and brush top with additional melted shortening. Cover with a clean tea towel; let rise in a warm place (80°–85° F.), free from drafts, until double in bulk. (As my Pennsylvania Dutch cousin says: "Johann, let double it rise, almost.")

Turn dough out on lightly floured board (mixing table or butcher's block is ideal) and shape into small balls about ½ inch in diameter. ("Desired size" is the way to state it, methinks, as I had an engineer friend measure them minutely, Ladies.) Place 2 or 3 balls in each well of greased muffin pans. (Pie pans are excellent with one in center; right, Grandmothers?) Brush with shortening and cover.

Let rise until double in bulk, as before. Bake in hot oven (400° F.) 15 to 20 minutes. Makes about 20 medium-sized rolls. (If desired, brush tops of baked rolls with butter or margarine; or, before baking, brush tops with egg whites.)

First rise: 1½ to 2 hours. *Second rise:* approximately 1 hour.

Braué's Potato Loaf*

Trail blazer, often baked on the trail for breadwinners and their families—but not for dieting!

To prepare: 25 minutes. *To heat:* 45 minutes. (Should be prepared a day in advance of eating.)

5 cups cubed cooked potatoes (6 medium-sized spuds)
3 tablespoons lard, butter, or margarine
1 cup flour (all-purpose)
1½ teaspoons salt
⅛ teaspoon black pepper

1 cup milk
1 tablespoon minced parsley
2 tablespoons chopped pimiento
2 tablespoons grated onion
1 cup (4 oz.) shredded sharp cheddar cheese

Grease bottom and sides of a loaf pan. Melt butter in saucepan. Blend in a mixture of flour, salt, and pepper; heat until mixture bubbles, stirring constantly, then remove from heat. Add milk gradually, stirring all the while. Bring rapidly to boiling; cook 1 to 2 minutes longer. Stir in the parsley, pimiento, and onion. Pour over cubed potatoes and toss lightly to mix thoroughly. Turn into prepared pan and chill in refrigerator overnight. (Needless to state, the pioneers used their ingenuity.)

Unmold potato loaf onto a buttered heatproof platter (steak platter) or leave in loaf pan. 'Tis good both ways! Heat in a 350° F. oven 30 minutes. Remove from oven; sprinkle cheese evenly on top of loaf. Return to oven and heat 15 minutes longer, or until cheese is melted. If you do not wish the cheese treatment, heat loaf a touch bit more than the 30 minutes. Energizing!

"Provision for others is a fundamental responsibility of human life."—WOODROW WILSON

Braué's Whole-Wheat (Graham) Bread*

4 tablespoons brown sugar
2 teaspoons salt
1½ cups milk, scalded
4 tablespoons melted shortening

2 cups starter or
1 cake yeast dissolved in
1½ cups lukewarm water
7 cups whole-wheat or graham flour (or a blend)

Stir sugar, salt, and shortening into scalded milk until dissolved. Cool to lukewarm. Add starter, or dissolve yeast in lukewarm water and add to cooled milk mixture. Stir in half the flour, beat until smooth. Gradually add remaining flour; mix well to form soft dough and knead on lightly floured board until smooth and satiny, using all-purpose flour. Shape dough into ball; place in greased bowl and brush top with additional melted shortening. Cover with towel; let rise in a warm place (80°–85° F.), free from drafts, until double in bulk.

Divide dough into 2 equal portions; shape into 2 loaves. Place in greased bread pans. Brush with shortening; cover, let rise until double in bulk, as before. Bake in 350° F. oven about 1 hour.

No frills here, just good ingredients, pleasant kitchen, workable tools!

Father's Bread

(Straight-Dough Method)

2 cups milk	2 cups water
¼ cup sugar	1 cake fast yeast
4 teaspoons salt	¼ cup lukewarm water
2 tablespoons shortening	7 cups flour (variable)

Scald milk. Add sugar, salt, shortening and water. Cool to lukewarm. Add yeast, which has been softened in ¼ cup lukewarm water. Add flour gradually, mixing it in thoroughly.

When dough is stiff, turn out on lightly floured board and knead until smooth and satiny. Shape into smooth ball. Place in greased bowl. Cover, and let rise in warm place, 82°–86° F., until doubled in bulk. Punch down. Let rise again.

When light and doubled in bulk, divide into equal portions. Shape each portion into a smooth ball; cover well and let rest 10 to 14 minutes. Mold into loaves. Place in greased bread pans. Bake in moderately hot oven, 400°–425° F. for 15 minutes; reduce heat to 350° F. for 40 minutes more.

This bread is guaranteed to disappear in a few minutes if buttered, sugared, cinnamoned, and toasted for boys!

"Everybody's business nobody's business."

Father's Sponge Method

As in most German home bakeries, the family lived over the bakery, and as a boy, I enjoyed the pleasant sounds those nights when my father put flour in the sponge, "Folla in da punch."

Use same proportions as in straight-dough recipe.

In a large bowl, soften 1 dry yeast cake in 2 cups of lukewarm liquid (water or potato water) for ½ hour, then stir in 4 cups of flour until batter thickens; beat until satiny-smooth (preferably with hands). Cover with a clean cloth, let rise in a warm place away from air currents overnight while you sleep, dreaming of golden-brown bread.

Sponge should be nice and bubbly, doubled in bulk, a beautiful sight to behold early in the morning! Punch and stir down the sponge with your hand, feeling the life of the sponge as millions have before: truly a revelation.

Scald 2 cups liquid, add the salt, sugar, and shortening; cool to lukewarm. Stir into sponge along with rest of flour. Mix thoroughly until dough does not stick to hands; then turn out on lightly floured board and continue as in straight-dough recipe.

This is quite an accomplishment . . . you should feel justly proud!

"Hope is the dream of the waking man."—ARISTOTLE

Braué's Golden-Brown Yeast Bread Challah

The Braués' wonderful Jewish friends, neighbors, and customers brought this into mouth-watering being.

2 packages dry yeast (or starter)
2 cups warm water
4 teaspoons salt
½ cup sugar

1¼ cups shortening, melted (vegetable or salad oil)
3 eggs, beaten (save a bit in bottom of cup)
7 cups all-purpose flour, sifted

Dissolve yeast in water in large bowl; let rest for a moment. Add salt, sugar, and shortening; blend in eggs and half the flour. Slowly add the rest of the flour, stir-stir-stir, until dough is stiff; turn out on lightly floured board, knead until satiny-smooth; place in a greased bowl. Cover with a clean cloth, let rise in a warm place, until doubled in bulk, over an hour.

Punch down, turn out on lightly floured board again; cut into equal portions, roll into strips about a foot and a half long. Braid strips and seal ends (3 per loaf), place on greased sheet or cookie pan, let rise for an hour, brush with "egg in bottom of cup" and bake in a 350° F. oven for an hour, until golden-brown.

"Art is man's nature, nature is God's art."—OWEN MEREDITH

Dad's Batter White Bread

No-knead enriched white bread. Dad taught a busy society lady how to bake this one, around the time enriched flour made its powdery appearance.

1 package dry yeast	2 tablespoons shortening
1¼ cups warm water	2 tablespoons sugar
2 teaspoons salt	3 cups enriched flour, sifted

Dissolve yeast in warm water; let it rest while you mix shortening, sugar, salt, and 1½ cups flour in a large mixing bowl. Add the yeast mixture, stirring constantly. Now beat vigorously by hand, or use an electric mixer at medium speed (by hand about 300 good mixing strokes; with mixer for 3 minutes). Please scrape bowl often for full mixing as you add remaining flour, blending and mixing until satiny-smooth.

Cover with a clean cloth; let rise in a warm place until doubled in bulk while you accomplish a few small chores or read a story to the little one(s).

Do not punch, but stir dough down; then spoon into bread pan(s). Sho' will be sticky, but pat top with a floured hand, as you would an obedient child; this will give loaf a semblance of shape.

Cover again, set in warm place, and let rise for another 30 minutes. Bake in a 375° F. oven for 45 minutes. Then place loaf on rack and brush top with melted butter. This is a beneficial recipe for beginners.

SMALL LOAVES. This would be an ideal mix for small bread pans for the small fry!

BATTER WHOLE-WHEAT BREAD. For a variation of the above recipe, add a touch of honey or molasses; flour count will be 2 cups white, 1 cup unsifted whole wheat.

"If a man bakes bread with indifference, he bakes a bitter loaf that feeds but half his hunger."—KAHLIL GIBRAN

Braué's Home Dairy Loaf

This one pleased the dairy farmers!

2 tablespoons dry yeast
4 cups water (110° F.)
1½ tablespoons salt
3 tablespoons dairy butter
2¼ tablespoons granulated
    sugar

¾ tablespoon country honey
2½ tablespoons whole egg
1 cup country milk
6 cups flour (stone-ground,
    preferably)

Dissolve yeast in water in large bowl; add salt, milk, sugar, honey, and all the rest of the ingredients, mixing well until satiny-smooth. Cover with clean cloth and let rise until doubled in size.

Turn out on lightly floured board, knead gently for a few moments, mold into balls, shape into loaves, and place into greased bread pans. Cover and let rise until dough is just above edge of pans; bake in 350° F. oven for an hour.

"We walk by Faith, not by sight."—The Bible

Braué's Healthful Schleswig-Holstein Whole-Wheat Bread

Dad's truly noble loaf—full of nutritional natural ingredients . . . an adventure in creativeness.

2 cups of your own starter (at room temperature) or
2 packages of yeast
4 cups of stock, warm (liquids that are abundantly rich in food
    value, potato water, soup water, scalded milk, etc.)
1 tablespoon salt (less, if stock is seasoned)
5 tablespoons honey (with comb, if desired)
¼ cup nutritional oil (if sesame butter is used, double portion)
3 tablespoons nutritional yeast(optional)
10 cups whole-wheat flour

Blend starter or yeast and half of stock in your large mixing bowl. Carefully add rest of ingredients except for half the flour, blending well. Cover and let rise for an hour.

Stir in rest of flour, mixing until stiff. Turn out on lightly floured board, knead until smooth. Place in greased bowl, turn over (dough, madam) once; cover, let rise for another good hour. Punch dough down; turn it out onto floured board. Cut in half, mold into loaves, place in greased pans, let rise (proof) until doubled. Bake in 350° F. oven for an hour.

A RAHN VARIATION. Add 3 eggs, beaten, to stock.

"Abstracted from home, I know no happiness in the world."
—THOMAS JEFFERSON

Braué's Dietary Whole-Wheat Bread

A professionally recommended favorite of the Braué Home Bakery clientele for generations.

2 cups of starter or
2 packages active dry yeast, dissolved in

4 cups milk, scalded, and
1 cup of potato water, lukewarm

Set aside while you blend all of the dry ingredients.

1 tablespoon salt
3 tablespoons soy flour
½ cup nutritional yeast
3 tablespoons bone meal
½ cup powdered milk
½ cup wheat germ

8 cups whole-wheat flour (variable)
6 tablespoons honey
6 tablespoons oil
1 cup porridge, cooked

Mix honey, oil, and porridge with yeast mixture; then incorporate with other ingredients until stiff and thoroughly blended. Turn out onto floured board, knead until "elastically smooth." Place in greased (oiled) bowl, turn dough over once, cover and let rise until doubled in bulk (at least an hour).

Punch down, turn out onto floured board, cut into thirds, mold into loaves, and place in oiled pans. Proof for a few moments (re-cover and let rest). Bake in 380° F. oven for a little over an hour (or at 380° F. for 12 minutes; then lower oven heat, and bake at 350° for 50 more minutes).

"Unkindness is no remedy at law."

Braué's Home-Baked Whole-Wheat Bread

Dad baked this zestful bread for an Ozark family, in baker's dozen lots of thirteen.

2 packages active dry yeast or
2 cakes compressed yeast
1 cup lukewarm water
½ cup brown sugar (firmly packed for measuring)

2 teaspoons salt
2 cups milk
7 cups whole-wheat flour
2 tablespoons melted shortening

If used, dissolve yeast in water, soften for 10 minutes. In the meantime, scald milk (until it puckers—do not boil), then add brown sugar and salt to milk. Combine yeast or starter and milk mixture in large bowl, stirring softly the while. Add 3 cups of flour, melted shortening, and mix thoroughly. Now mix in the remaining flour, a little at a time, until dough does not "stick."

Turn dough out on lightly floured bread board, and knead hard for better bread texture, until springy-smooth. Shape with hands into ball, place dough into greased bowl, turn dough over once, cover with a clean cloth, and place in your bread-warming place.

Let dough rise until double in size; then punch it down with your fists. Lovingly lift up the dough; place it on lightly floured board, and let it rest for a verse of "Let Us Break Bread Together!"

Cut dough in half, shape into two loaves (or into quarters), place in greased bread pans, and brush with melted butter or shortening. Cover with clean cloth and let rise again until size is doubled—nearly an hour.

Bake in a 380°–400° F. oven for 10 minutes; reduce heat to 350°–370° F. and continue baking for 40 minutes, at which time the loaves will tumble out of their pans ready for your anticipating family!

"Gie your tongue mair holidays than your head."—Scottish (or rather, A GUD SCOTSMAN)

Father's General Grenville M. Dodge Cracked-Wheat Bread

Named after the Great Council Bluffs engineer of transcontinental railroad fame and President Lincoln's friend. This loaf made many friends in the Lincoln High Bluff area.

2 packages active dry yeast
1 cup warm water
1 cup milk, scalded
1 teaspoon salt
2 tablespoons butter, margarine, oil, or other shortening
¼ cup molasses

1 cup cold water
1 cup cracked wheat* (soak in cup of cold water overnight)
6 cups all-purpose flour (another good chance to blend your flours)

Dissolve yeast in warm water in a large mixing bowl. In another bowl pour the milk over butter, molasses, and cracked-wheat mixture, stiring until lukewarm; then combine with yeast and water, stirring the while. Gradually add half the flour and beat for 3 minutes; then add the rest of flour (needed) to make a stiff dough.

Turn out onto lightly floured board and knead until satiny-smooth (12 minutes). Place in greased bowl, turn once, cover with a clean cloth, and place in a warm spot. Let rise until doubled in bulk. (This one will rise faster, a bit over 35 minutes.)

Punch down, shape into loaves, place in greased bread pans or your favorite baking containers. Bake in 375° F. oven for nearly 10 minutes, lower heat to 350° and bake for 40 more minutes. Remove from pans to rack, cool.

"There is hardly anything in the world that someone cannot make a little worse and sell a little cheaper, and the people who consider price alone are this man's lawful prey."—JOHN RUSKIN

---

* Cracked wheat is the cracked and cleaned whole kernel of wheat.

Dad's Hawkeye Graham Bread

A depression-day favorite ... five cents a loaf ... "barter bread."

2 packages active dry yeast
1 cup water
2 cups milk, scalded
4 teaspoons salt
¼ cup shortening
¼ cup honey

2 cups water, cold
3 cups graham flour, unsifted
5 cups all-purpose flour,
    blended with the graham
    flour

Dissolve yeast in warm water in large mixing bowl. In another bowl, combine milk, honey, salt, and shortening; stir, then add the cold water. Stir until smooth.

Gradually add the flour blend, beat until stiff (but workable). Turn out onto floured board, knead until dough is "springy to touch."

Place dough in greased bowl, turn over once, cover, and let rise for an hour (until doubled).

Punch dough down, turn out to floured board, cut into desired portions, shape into loaves, and place in greased bread pans. Cover and let rise for a bit over 30 minutes. Bake in 450° F. oven for 10 minutes; lower heat to 350° F. and continue baking for a little more than 30 minutes more.

"Be silent or speak something worth hearing."

Braué's Old-fashioned Wheat Bread

A sunny loaf, handed down to Mother. It was once a peace offering to the great Sioux braves when they came a-visiting our Black Hill friends long ago. Those were the days when a bear skin on the roof or door meant "Friends of the Indian."

1 cake yeast (or 2 cups
    starter)
¼ cup lukewarm water
2 cups milk, scalded
4 tablespoons dark syrup
    (sorghum)

2½ teaspoons salt
1 tablespoon shortening
4 cups whole-wheat flour
    (preferably ground in your
    kitchen, or stone-ground)

Dissolve yeast in water, for leavening, and set aside while in large bowl you mix milk, syrup, salt, and shortening. Set aside to cool. Mix and add the yeast mixture to the milk mixture, plus almost all the flour. For "not to stick to your hands or elbows" consistency, add a little white flour. Place dough in greased bowl, cover with clean cloth, und in der varm plaze geputten for 2 hours.

Punch down; let rise again until almost doubled. Divide with sharp knife or cutter, knead (with both hands) on floured board until "soft-smooth." Round dough, shape into loaves, and place in greased pans. Cover and let rise until doubled.

Bake in 425° F. oven for 15 minutes; lower heat to 375° F. and bake for approximately an hour. These will keep well, if kept out of the reach of sons, daughters, husband, and in-laws!

"A noble mind disdains not to repent."—HOMER

Braué's Wheaten Bread

The following recipe was, and still is, a great energizing favorite of the Nordic Iowa farmers.

3 tablespoons dry yeast
3 cups water (110° F.)
2 teaspoons salt
3 cups whole-wheat flour
  (bran or graham)
4 cups all-purpose flour

¼ cup brown sugar
1 tablespoon dark molasses
3 tablespoons dairy butter
½ cup milk (nonfat), scalded
¼ cup wheat germ

Dissolve yeast in water in large bowl; add milk, salt, sugar, molasses, butter, stirring constantly. After blending flours and wheat germ well, add to liquid mixture; mix until smooth.

Cover with a clean cloth; let rise in a warm place until doubled in bulk. Turn out onto a lightly floured board, and knead well for a few moments. Do not mold into balls, but shape into loaves; place in greased bread pans; cover; let rise for 30 minutes. Bake in 350° F. oven for 1 hour.

"In a calm sea every man is a pilot."—Old German saying

Mrs. Don G. Merritt's Swiss Bread

Grossvate Bleiker, Mrs. Merritt's grandfather, lived in a small Swiss village near the German border. The baker, who lived atop a hill, one day loaded his cart with round loaves of this bread when the inevitable happened. The two-wheeled cart turned over, and all the round loaves rolled down the hill with the baker close behind in pursuit, loudly demanding that the loaves halt their untimely flight.

1 cup of your favorite starter, or
1 tablespoon of active dry yeast dissolved in:
2 cups of warm water
Thoroughly mix with:
3 cups rye flour (meal, or a mixture of dark flours)

Reserve this starter by placing in jar and refrigerate. In mixing bowl thoroughly mix together—

1 cup sugar
1 quart warm water
4 cups all-purpose flour (unbleached white)

Cover with a warm cloth, and set overnight in a warm place. On der gut morgen, take 1 cup of starter, add a bit of sugar to it, spoon starter mix into overnight mix (after you have punched it down). Add and thoroughly mix the following to your overnight-starter batch:

3 teaspoons salt
1 cup of shortening or oil
7 cups all-purpose flour

Turn out on lightly floured board (table); knead for 12 minutes. Cover, let rise until doubled. Shape into round or long loaves, place on greased sheets (or earthen tile), bake in 375° F. oven for 1 hour.

*"When the movement is forward, no man can afford to fix his constant gaze upon what lies behind. 'It might have been' is the cry of the lost soul, but what might yet be in spite of all the past errors and mistakes is worth living and working for. Forget what can't be helped and live for what can be helped."—*GRIFF

Braué's Golden-Heart Bread

Dad really believed in this nutritional recipe, for it had a rich flavor all its own.

1 package dry yeast
¼ cup lukewarm water
2 teaspoons salt
2 cups boiling water
2 tablespoons sugar

2 tablespoons shortening
5 cups sifted all-purpose flour
2½ cups wheat germ
3 cups nonfat dry milk solids*

Dissolve yeast in the lukewarm water. In a large bowl, pour the boiling water and dry milk (remember homogenized milk is richer, so please use less than nonfat), mixing with egg beater, electric mixer, spoon, or by hand. (Mixing by hand, feeling the life-giving batch in your palms, mixing with vigor all the while, is still the one better method; 'tis difficult, though.) Then stir in shortening, sugar, and salt, mixing constantly and well; let cool to lukewarm.

Now your interest should mount. Add the softened yeast and half the sifted flour into the milk mixture and stir well; then add the wheat germ plus enough of the remaining flour to realize a soft, satiny-smooth dough. Please add more flour, if necessary, but be ever watchful in this operation.

Place dough on lightly floured board, and cover with bowl (try this on other breads, too); then you both rest for 10 minutes. Knead dough until baby-smooth and elastic; cut dough with sharp knife or cutter, shape into balls, cover again with bowls or cloth, and let rest another 10 minutes. Shape into loaves and place, seam down, in bread pans. Lightly grease tops of loaves, cover with clean cloth, and let rise in a warm place until doubled in bulk, almost 90 minutes. Place in a 350° F. oven and bake for 50 minutes. Remove from pans and cool on rack.

"Accept the challenge of Life—use your God-given talents."

---

* If we haven't mentioned dry milk before, please forgive, for it serves well.

Grossmutter's Golden-Sunrise Wheat or Oatmeal Brot

*Dutch, German, and Austrian cooking-baking seems to go on for-
ever . . . You are bound to remember your grandmother, or someone's warm-hearted Deutsche Grossmutter, baking in a happy-
aromatic, love-abounding kitchen!*

2 packages active dry yeast
(or 2 cakes compressed
yeast)
¼ cup warm water
1 tablespoon salt
2 cups milk
¼ cup honey

2 tablespoons shortening
4 cups all-purpose flour
2 cups granulated whole-
wheat cereal, uncooked, or
2 cups uncooked rolled oats,
preferably the quick-cooking
kind

Dissolve yeast in warm water in large bowl. Scald milk,
honey, shortening, and salt in small saucepan, then set aside and
cool to lukewarm. Stir these two mixtures together in a large
bowl. Stir in half of flour, beating or stirring until mixture is
satiny-smooth. Stir in whole-wheat (oatmeal) cereal, then add
enough of remaining flour to make a nice, stiff dough. Turn out
onto lightly floured board or table and knead thoroughly until
dough is elastically smooth; then return to bowl, brush top with
shortening or oil, and cover with a clean cloth.

Let rise in a warm place for 45 minutes until doubled in
size. Now punch down dough, cut into desired sizes for loaves
(a candy-making and baking scale is a must if you become
imbued with the "joy of baking" routine) and knead, a few
times at slow tempo, on lightly floured board. Shape into round
loaves.

Place on greased baking sheet. Cut your favorite symbol on
top of loaves (knife must be sharp); let rise again in your
favorite warm spot during your favorite 30-minute program.
Bake in a 375° F. oven for just short of 1 hour; cool on racks.

Makes a wonderful gift for a new neighbor or friend. But
patience is the word!

"The wise distrust the unknown."—LEE FONTAINE

Braué's Basic White Bread Recipe

When you have become proficient with the no-knead recipe, please try this good mix. You will be pleasantly surprised.

1 package active dry yeast
¼ cup water (warm for dry yeast, lukewarm for compressed yeast)
2 teaspoons salt

2 cups milk, scalded
¼ cup butter or margarine
2 teaspoons sugar
6 cups sifted all-purpose flour (or enriched)

Dissolve yeast in water; let stand while you mix milk, sugar, salt and butter in a large bowl. Let stand until lukewarm, then add yeast mixture and 3 cups of flour. Beat until flour has disappeared; then add remaining flour, stirring-mixing constantly. Turn out on floured board. Knead until satiny-smooth. Place in greased bowl, turn over once, cover with a clean cloth; then let rise in a warm place for 90 minutes until doubled in size.

Punch dough down; cover again and let rise for 30 minutes. Cut with sharp knife or cutter, shape into loaves and expectantly place them into greased bread pans. Cover with another clean cloth; let rise until doubled and bake in a 400° F. oven for a touch bit over 30 minutes.

(On the last adding of flour, add 1 cup of seedless raisins and a smidgen of cinnamon. The male members of your family will love you for this loaf of goodness!)

VARIATIONS. For pan rolls that melt in one's mouth, use the Basic White Bread Recipe. At first rising, cut half the dough into small pieces, about 12 to 16. Shape into balls, place close together on greased cookie pan, cover with clean cloth, let rise for 30 minutes, brush with melted butter, and bake in 425° F. oven for nearly 25 minutes. Serve hot with country butter and preserves!

What to do with the rest of this batch? Cut dough into a number of pieces and roll-shape into bread sticks; place on greased sheet or pan, cover, and let rise for 30 minutes. Bake in 400° F. oven for 15 minutes. *Wunderbar* with salads and Latin dishes!

Here's the one the men will demand to supplement their cookouts. Mix the following in the Basic White Bread Recipe mix: 2 teaspoons caraway seeds, 1 teaspoon leaf sage, and ¼ teaspoon nutmeg; follow the recipe up to the shaping. Now cut into pieces, shape into sticks, place on greased sheets. Cover and let rise for 30 to 45 minutes. Bake in 400° F. oven 15 to 20 minutes and cool. Mmm, what taste!

"The discontented man finds no easy chair."—FRANKLIN

Even a busy person can bake delicious bread. Bake these aromatic taste delights on week ends, holidays, while the family is out, and use the dough-rising times for household chores, phone calls, and the Sunday-school lesson.

Dad's New-Era White Bread

Just before Dad passed away, Christmas, 1940, the new enriched flour came into being, and the following recipe is the result, after many nights of work and experimentation. A one-pound loaf sold for five cents!

2 yeast cakes or 2 packages dry yeast
¼ cup lukewarm water
1 quart scalded milk (good spot to economize with powdered milk)
½ cup shortening (almost-about, 1 cup for rolls)
2 heaping tablespoons salt
½ cup sugar
11 cups sifted enriched white flour

Soften yeast in lukewarm water. Place milk, shortening (try corn oil some time), salt, and sugar in a large mixing bowl and wait until it is lukewarm; then add softened yeast mixture. Stir until well mixed. Add 4 cups sifted flour and stir until thoroughly mixed. Cover with clean cloth, place in fairly warm place, and let rise for about 30 minutes. Then remove cloth and add remaining flour and mix well.

Turn the dough onto floured board and knead until satiny-smooth, about 10 minutes. Round dough into smooth ball and place in a large bowl. Cover with clean cloth, place in a warm spot away from drafts, and allow to rise until double in bulk, approximately 2 hours.

Punch dough down and cut in half (dough cutter), then each portion half again. Mold into loaves and place each loaf into a greased bread pan. Cover with a clean cloth and let loaves rise until double in bulk, about 1 hour.

Bake loaves one hour: 375° F. for 15 minutes; 350° F. for 30 minutes, und off der heat for der last 15 minutes.

"Who can enjoy alone?"—MILTON

Grossmutter's Butter-Bran Bread

To escape the Prussianism of the nineteenth century, Grandmother Rahn brought nine children over in steerage, plus several tantalizing recipes, this being one.

1 package active dry yeast or
2 cups starter
2 cups warm water, 112° F.
2 teaspoons salt
2 cups boiling water
1 cup whole bran

3 tablespoons butter
3 tablespoons dark-brown sugar
2 tablespoons molasses
8 cups all-purpose flour

Soften yeast in warm water and let it stand. Thoroughly blend bran, butter, sugar, molasses, boiling water, and salt in a large bowl; then set aside to cool until lukewarm. Blend 1 cup of flour and the yeast mixture into the bran bowl and beat (stir) until satiny-smooth.

Gradually add some of the remaining flour until you have beaten the mixture into a doughy smoothness, both soft and light! Turn twice in greased bowl, cover with clean cloth or apron, and let rise in the homey warm corner until doubled in size. Turn out onto a lightly floured surface. Cut into two or more portions, and shape dough into loaves. Put into greased loaf pans, cover, let rise in your favorite warm place until double der dough is.

Place in a 325° F. oven for an hour. Then you may remove the loaves and lightly brush them with melted butter or your favorite topping. Now stand off a bit and marvel at your handiwork!

"Using and enjoying is true having."—WHICHCOTE

Braué's Old-fashioned Pioneer-Trail White Bread

A good basic recipe—a perfect blend of Old Country fact and midwestern lore.

1 cup starter	1 tablespoon salt
1 pint milk	1 tablespoon lard (shortening
1 pint boiling water	or butter)
2 tablespoons sugar	3 quarts flour, warmed
pinch of soda	

The boiling water and milk should be mixed with the sugar and half of the flour. By this time, when the flour is well beaten, add the starter. Cover with a clean cloth and set in a warm place for 30 minutes.

Add the remainder of the flour with the soda, shortening, and salt. Mix this up real well. Turn out on a lightly floured board and knead until stiff. Cover and set away in a warm place until doubled in bulk. Turn it out again on a floured board and knead lightly; let dough rest for a spell.

Cut into equal portions; form or mold into individual loaves. Place in greased pans and bake for 50 minutes in a 350° F. oven.

(If a cup of the flour is scalded and added to this batch, the bread will be ready for the oven in less time.)

You can increase the nutritional value of your white bread or rolls with this hint: place 1 tablespoon soy flour, 1 tablespoon nonfat dry milk, and 1 teaspoon wheat germ in the bottom of each cup of flour. If you cannot procure these ingredients, don't give up. Just contact your pharmacist or health-food store.

Tante Carrie's Home-Hearty Bread

A milk and honey loaf as healthful as can be!

2 packages quick dry yeast	1 tall can evaporated milk plus
1 cup warm water	skim milk, but no shortening
1 tablespoon salt	10 cups all-purpose (or en-
¼ cup honey	riched) flour

Dissolve yeast in 1 cup of water in small bowl. Set aside while you heat (do not boil) honey, salt, and a tablespoon of water; then add, while stirring, the evaporated milk.

Fill empty milk can with skim milk; add to liquid mixture, stirring all the while. Pour this healthful liquid mixture into a large bowl; then add the yeast mixture and 4 cups of flour, and beat until satiny-smooth. Cover with a clean cloth and let rise in a warm place for about 2 hours.

Add the remaining flour, mix thoroughly, let rise again until doubled in bulk. Turn out onto lightly floured board and knead gently but well. Place in greased bowl; cover with a clean cloth, and let rise again until almost doubled in bulk.

Punch down, knead, and shape into loaves. Fit into large greased bread pans (9½ by 5¼ by 2¾ inches), cover and let rise for 30 minutes. Bake just under 1 hour in a 375° F. oven.

"Nothing astonishes men as much as common sense and plain-dealing."—RALPH WALDO EMERSON

Braué Home Bakery's Quick Hundred-Per-Cent Whole-Wheat Bread

Baked exclusively for the Iowa farmer!

2 packages quick dry yeast
2 tablespoons brewers' yeast
3 cups warm water
4 teaspoons salt
¼ cup molasses
¼ cup brown sugar

1 cup nonfat dry milk
3 tablespoons wheat germ
3 tablespoons softened shortening (or corn oil)
7 cups whole-wheat flour (½ cup soy flour for nutrition)

Dissolve the dry yeast in the warm water in a large bowl. Add molasses and brown sugar, stirring easily; then let stand while in another bowl you blend flour, dry milk, wheat germ, brewer's yeast, and salt—stir and sift, sift and stir. Add shortening to yeast mixture, and immediately mix both mixtures and beat vigorously until you are satisfied 'tis satiny-smooth.

Turn into 2 greased loaf pans, and let rise about 30 minutes. Bake in a 375° F. oven for a good 50 minutes.

Uncle Gerhard's Onion Bread

A Prussian prize of war!

1 package dry yeast (or 1 cup starter)
2 cups warm water
1 tablespoon instant minced onion (or chopped onion)
2 tablespoons sugar
2 tablespoons salt (or celery salt or seasoned salt)
2 tablespoons shortening (or oil or butter)
½ teaspoon oregano, crushed
6 cups all-purpose flour
1 Bermuda onion, peeled and sliced into separate rings
2 tablespoons melted butter (or oil or margarine)

Dissolve the yeast in the warm water in a large mixing bowl. In another mixing bowl, add minced onion, sugar, salt, shortening, oregano, and half the flour. Blend well, add to the yeast mixture, and beat at medium speed with your mixer or with fast strokes by hand—at least 300 of them. Stir in the remaining flour.

Cover and let rise for about an hour, then beat with a spoon for 1 moment. Pour into greased bread pan. Pat the top of the dough with a lightly floured hand to level it off. Cover and let rise for 30 minutes; then dip the onion rings into the melted butter or the oil and place on top of the loaf.

Bake in a 375° F. oven for 40 minutes. Remove from the pan and cool on rack.

Braué's Exotic Onion Bread

A family favorite for centuries.

1 package active dry yeast
¼ cup water
¼ cup lukewarm water
4 tablespoons dried minced onion
2 cups milk
2 tablespoons shortening
2 tablespoons sugar
2 teaspoons salt
6 cups sifted flour (you can experiment here with different flours)
1 teaspoon celery salt
½ teaspoon poultry seasoning

Soften onion and ¼ cup water in small bowl; let stand. Dissolve yeast in ¼ cup lukewarm water in a large bowl; let stand. Scald milk in a saucepan and stir in the shortening, sugar, and salt. Cool to lukewarm and stir into softened-yeast bowl.

Sift the celery salt and poultry seasoning with 3 cups of flour, stir into yeast mixture, and beat until smooth. Add the softened onion mixture and more flour until dough is stiff.

Knead dough on a floured board for approximately 10 minutes. Place dough in a greased bowl, then turn completely over for top-surface greasing. Cover with a clean cloth and let stand in a warm spot until dough is doubled. Punch down and let dough rest in bowl for 12 to 15 minutes.

Roll out on a floured board ("turn out" is the proper phrase, but then that is too military all the time, *nicht wahr?*), and form into two loaves—more if for smaller pans. Place in loaf pans, cover with a dry cloth, let rise in a warm place until double in size.

Bake in a 400° F. oven about 40 minutes. Place on cooling rack, but it won't last long there! Good toasted, too!

Dad's Campout Potato Bread
Perfect for Scouts or the family outing.

1 tablespoon dry yeast, or
2 cups starter
2 cups milk, lukewarm
1 tablespoon salt
1 tablespoon sugar

1 tablespoon shortening
6 cups whole-wheat or unbleached white flour
½ cup potato flour

Dissolve 1 tablespoon dry yeast in (or add 2 cups starter to) lukewarm milk. Add salt, sugar, and shortening. Mix well and add wheat flour and potato flour. Blend and mix until smooth, smooth, smooth.

Cover and let rise for 2 hours. Punch down and fold over dough; let rise for 10 more minutes. Shape into loaves and rolls and bake in your Dutch oven for 50 minutes 350° F.

Potato flour is now a good substitute for freshly cooked potatoes because of its uniformity, and as a conditioner of dough. Use 4 parts milk to 1 part potato flour.

Rahn-Braué's Home Bread

All of Grossmutter's girls—Daughters and friends—baked this dandy.

3 cups compressed yeast, or
3 envelopes active dry yeast, or
2 cups starter
2 cups lukewarm water
¼ cup sugar

2 cups milk, scalded
2 tablespoons salt
4 tablespoons shortening
2 cups cold water
12 cups all-purpose flour (or a blend of flours)

If used, dissolve yeast in warm water in a large mixing bowl. In another mixing bowl, blend shortening, sugar, salt, and milk; add cold water last. Let this stand for a few moments while everything becomes room temperature. Combine with the yeast mixture or starter. Add flour gradually and mix well. Beat for at least 3 minutes; then gradually add more flour until you have the correct consistency.

Beat well all the time. Turn out on a floured board, and knead for 15 minutes, until the dough is "elastically smooth and alive." Divide into 6 portions. Cover and let rest for 15 minutes.

Mold; then shape into 6 loaves, and place them in greased square loaf pans. Bake in a 450° F. oven for an hour. Turn out of pans and cool upside down until you can't stand it any more and must have a slice.

Rahn-Braué Home Porridge

For any bread mix—1 cup into a batch of bread. Use as stock, whey, moisture, or healthful ingredient.

2 cups corn meal
½ cup soy grits
1 teaspoon salt

2 tablespoons nutritional yeast
1 cup potato water
3 cups hot potato water

Mix thoroughly corn meal, soy grits (or grits of your choice), salt, and nutritional yeast with 1 cup of potato water (or milk or water) until gooey.

Spoon this mixture into top of double boiler that contains 3 cups of hot potato water (or milk or water), and cook over direct heat for at least 5 minutes, stirring the while. Cover mit der cover yedt, und plaze over der bottom of double boiler filled with hot water. Cook slowly for an hour. Reserve in refrigerator; use as needed.

"A father is a banker provided by nature."—French saying

Rahn Family Old-Country Porridge Bread

A timeless favorite.

2 packages active dry yeast (or starter, homemade, or compressed yeast)
1 cup warm water (or stock, milk)
1 cup water, boiling
2 cups porridge, whey (or quick-cooking oatmeal, breakfast food, Cream of Wheat, etc.)
¼ cup shortening (or oil or butter)
½ cup molasses (or honey or syrup)
1 tablespoon salt
2 eggs, beaten
8 cups all-purpose flour (variable, or a blend of flours)
oil or melted butter (nutritional oil, if wished)
rolled oats or bran

Dissolve yeast in warm water in large mixing bowl. Set aside. In another bowl combine boiling water, porridge, shortening, molasses, and salt.

When lukewarm, gradually add eggs and half the flour; beat until blended. Add to yeast mixture; beat well while mixing in the remaining flour. Beat until stiff but pliable.

Turn out onto lightly-floured board (or table or canvas-covered work area). Cut dough in half, round into balls, place on greased baking tin (or cake pan, earthenware), cover and let rise for 2 hours. Brush tops of loaves with melted butter; sprinkle with oats. Bake in 350° F. oven for 50 minutes; remove to racks to cool.

My Uncle John's Hundred-Per-Cent Whole-Wheat Bread

Made from unbleached wheat flour, this is a truly nutritional, neighborly loaf—my uncle's favorite.

2 packages active dry yeast
1 cup water, warm
3 teaspoons salt
¼ cup molasses (honey, syrup, or beet sugar)
¼ cup shortening (oil, butter, margarine)
2 cups milk, scalded
8 cups 100-per-cent whole-wheat flour (unsifted)

Dissolve the yeast in warm water in large mixing bowl. Set aside and in another bowl incorporate milk, shortening, molasses, and salt and stir until smooth. Gradually pour this mixture into the yeast-mixture bowl and stir. Add half the flour; stir until smooth. Beat for 2 or 3 minutes. Add the remaining flour; beat until stiff—a dough that can be worked very well.

Turn out onto floured board and knead for 12 minutes, or until the dough springs back at the touch of a finger. Place the dough in a greased bowl. Cover with a clean cloth and let rise in warm place (85° F.) between 40 and 60 minutes. Punch the dough down.

Cut the dough in 3 equal portions and shape into loaves. Place in greased bread pans. Cover and let rise 30 to 40 minutes. Bake in a 425° F. oven for 12 minutes. Lower heat to 350° and bake for at least 30 more minutes. Brush the tops of the bread with butter or oil and cool in the pans for just a few moments before turning out on cooling racks.

Dad's Honey of an Egg—Whole-Wheat Bread

A delightful concoction calling for experimentation with flours, herbs, raisins, and spices, if desired.

1 package active dry yeast
1 cup warm water
1 cup milk, scalded
2 teaspoons salt, mixed with
6 cups whole-wheat flour
¼ cup honey
4 tablespoons cold-pressed soy oil
3 eggs, beaten

Dissolve yeast in warm water in large mixing bowl; set aside. Mix milk (lukewarm), eggs, and oil; pour into yeast water, and stir while you gradually add the flour-salt mixture. Mix well, until dough is spongy-soft.

Place in greased bowl, cover with a clean cloth, and let rise in warm place until doubled.

Turn out onto floured board, knead for five minutes, shape into loaves, and place in greased pans. Bake in a 350° F. oven for 50 minutes.

Rahn Family Old-Country Whole-Wheat Bread

Rich in health and heritage.

First the sponge:

1 package active dry yeast, or
1 cup starter
2 cups warm water
2 teaspoons salt

2 tablespoons sugar
4 cups all-purpose flour (variable, or a blend of unbleached and white flours)

An hour later:

¼ cup shortening
½ cup molasses (or honey, syrup)

1 cup boiling water
4 cups whole-wheat flour (variable)

Dissolve yeast in warm water in a large mixing bowl, add salt, sugar, and white flour. Stir and beat until smooth.

Cover and let rise until it is a "spongy sponge" (nearly an hour). To boiling water in another bowl add, stirring, shortening and molasses. Cool to lukewarm while you stir sponge down, adding the whole-wheat flour, then the molasses mixture, beating thoroughly.

Turn out onto lightly floured board; knead 6 minutes. Place in greased bowl, turn dough once, cover with a damp cloth, let rise for nearly 2 hours. Punch dough down, turn out onto a lightly floured board. Cut dough in portions, shape into loaves, place in greased loaf pans. Cover and let rise for an hour.

Bake in a 375° F. oven for 50 minutes. Remove from pans and cool on racks.

Braué's Herb Batter Bread

Remember, batter breads are easy to fix, but they are much coarser in appearance than kneaded breads; this healthful loaf has a distinctive flavor.

1 package active dry yeast
2 cups warm water (or stock)
2 teaspoons salt
2 tablespoons sugar

5 cups sifted all-purpose flour
1 teaspoon poultry seasoning
2 teaspoons caraway seed
½ teaspoon ground nutmeg

2 tablespoons soft shortening (or oil)

Dissolve yeast in water in large bowl. Stir in shortening, salt, sugar, and about half the flour; beat for about 3 minutes. Add the poultry seasoning, caraway seed, nutmeg, and the rest of the flour; beat until satiny-smooth.

Cover with a clean cloth, and let rise in a warm place until doubled in bulk (½ hour, usually). Stir with enthusiastic vigor and pour into greased loaf pan, cover, and again let rise until it appears doubled in size. Bake in a 400° F. oven for 40 minutes or until well-browned. Place on rack to cool.

Braué's Sharp-Cheese Batter Bread

Has the fine old-fashioned flavor of kneaded bread, but with the ease of "stir and pour."

1 package active dry yeast
1 cup warm water
1 teaspoon salt
1 tablespoon sugar

1 cup milk (your choice of type for richness' sake)
½ teaspoon paprika
5 cups all-purpose flour

1 cup grated sharp cheddar (or American) cheese

Dissolve yeast in water in large bowl. Stir in milk, salt, sugar, paprika, and almost half of flour; beat about 3 minutes. Stir in cheese and remaining flour and beat until satiny-smooth. Cover with a clean cloth, place in warm place, and let rise until batter is double the size (30 minutes).

Stir for a slow count of ten, then pour into greased loaf pan. Cover, and again let rise in warm place until batter rises to top of pan. Bake in a 375° F. oven for an hour; to rack, brush with butter or oil, then cool.

Grossmutter Rahn's Cheese Anadama Bread

Our grandmother's other version of this lovely mix, handed down from matriarch to eldest daughter.

1 package active dry yeast
1 cup warm water
½ cup yellow corn meal
3 teaspoons salt
2 tablespoons shortening

2 cups honey
2 cups sharp cheddar cheese, shredded (or your favorite; nearly ½ pound)
3 cups water

Combine corn meal, salt, shortening, honey, and cheese with 3 cups water in a saucepan over an even fire, stirring until bubbly-thick.

2 tablespoons butter, soft (or your choice of spread)
2 tablespoons paprika
1 tablespoon butter, melted

7 cups all-purpose flour (or a blend)
corn meal, at ready position

Dissolve yeast in warm water in large mixing bowl. Stir in corn-meal–cheese mixture and gradually add flour. Beat until blended and stiff but easy to handle. Turn out onto floured table or board and knead until satiny-smooth.

Place in a greased bowl, turn over once, and cover with a damp cloth. Let rise in a warm place for a bit over 1 hour. Punch down; let rise again for around 30 minutes.

Turn out on floured board and cut dough in half. Roll out half the dough into rectangle (9 by 12 inches), pressing out bubbles. Spread half the soft butter over dough and sprinkle with half the paprika. Roll up in jelly-roll fashion (9 inch end), sealing as you go along ("roll and seal"); pinch the end result to seal fully. Place the creased (long sealed) side down in greased bread pan, brush top of loaf with melted butter and sprinkle with corn meal.

Repeat with other half of dough, butter, and paprika.

Cover with a damp cloth, and let rise for nearly 1 hour. Bake in a 350° F. oven for almost 1 hour (browned well); remove to racks for cooling.

Grossmutter Rahn's Anadama Bread

One of the most popular and memorable of homemade breads.

1 package active dry (or compressed) yeast
2 cups warm water
3 tablespoons shortening
½ cup molasses
3 teaspoons salt

½ cup corn meal, soaked 1 hour or overnight in
1 cup tap water
3 cups whole-wheat flour blended well with
3 cups all-purpose flour

Dissolve yeast in warm water in large mixing bowl. Set aside while you blend flours or prepare your working space. Mix the remaining ingredients, gradually adding the flour, into the yeast-water mixture until nice and smooth.

Turn out onto a lightly floured surface, knead until smooth-elastic. Turn over once in greased bowl, cover, and let rise until doubled in bulk. Punch down lightly, knead gently, mold into loaves (or roll into round loaves for hearth bread).

Place into greased bread pans, bake in a 400° F. oven for 15 minutes; then lower to 375° F. and continue baking for nearly 40 minutes more.

"Open rebuke is better than secret hate."

Mother's Summery Orange Bread

A remarkable, exciting creation which produced lively and varied remarks in kitchen and gatherings.

1 cake or package yeast (or 1 cup starter)
1 cup orange juice (fresh, concentrate, or canned), lukewarm for cake, warm for package yeast
2 tablespoons sugar
1 tablespoon butter (or oil)
1 teaspoon salt
1 teaspoon orange rind, grated
4 cups all-purpose flour, variable (or your blend of flours, the biblical seven-grains mix)
¼ cup candied orange peel, shredded (optional)

Dissolve yeast in orange juice and sugar, stir. Gradually add the remaining ingredients, except candied orange peel (incorporating these ingredients beforehand iss most goot), beating well.

Cover, let rise until doubled, and turn out onto floured board. Knead in candied orange peel. Let rest for 6 minutes. Shape into loaf, place in greased bread pan, let rise for a spell. Bake in 375° F. oven for 40 minutes. Turn onto rack to cool.

"Many receive advice: only the wise profit by it."—SYRUS

Mother's Old-Country Tomato Bread

An impressive work of art that will disappear quickly to appear again and again "relishingly."

1 package yeast (or 1 cup starter)	1 teaspoon salt
1 cup warm water	1 cup tomato juice, scalded
1 tablespoon shortening	4 cups all-purpose flour, variable (or a blend of flours)
2 tablespoons sugar	

Dissolve yeast in water. In another bowl, thoroughly incorporate the shortening, sugar, salt, and tomato juice. Cool to lukewarm and add to yeast water, stirring well. Gradually add half the flour, beating well. Add the rest of the flour, mixing well.

Turn out on lightly floured board and knead for at least five minutes. Place in greased bowl, turn dough over once, and cover with clean cloth. Let rise in warm place for two hours. Turn out on lightly floured board, shape into loaf (or two small loaves), place in greased bread pan, brush top with melted shortening (or oil or lard).

Cover and let rise until doubled. Bake in 400° F. oven for 15 minutes; then lower oven heat and bake in 375° oven for remainder of hour.

"Parents are the trunks of trees, children the branches, but grandparents are the roots." Lost, and again found, each generation.

Mrs. Gruber's Egg-Cinnamon Bread

Baked originally by the Braué Home Bakery for this nice family
who lived near Indian Creek.

1 package active dry or compressed yeast
2 tablespoons lukewarm water
1 teaspoon salt
⅔ cup milk
½ cup sugar

6 tablespoons margarine
2 eggs
3 cups sifted all-purpose flour
1½ teaspoons cinnamon
2 tablespoons melted butter or
margarine, or egg white

Dissolve yeast in water and let stand while you scald the
milk. In a large bowl pour milk over ¼ cup sugar, salt, and about
4 tablespoons margarine. Set aside to cool to lukewarm; then
add eggs, yeast, and half the flour, beating the while until satiny
smooth. Mix and beat in the remaining flour with a large spoon.

Cover with a clean cloth, in der varm bplazce geputten; let
rise until doubled in size.

Punch down and knead lightly. Roll out onto lightly floured
board, spread with remaining 2 tablespoons butter or margarine,
sprinkle with remaining sugar and cinnamon, roll up tightly
from end to end and place in greased bread pan. Brush with 2
tablespoons melted butter and let rise until doubled in size,
about 45 minutes. Bake in a 350° F. oven for about 30 minutes.
Cool, if you can!

"Do the headwork before the handwork."

Braué Home Bakery Spiral Bread Dough

Filled with the wonderful world of fillings—your favorites and
ours.

2 packages active dry yeast
1 cup warm water
1 cup milk, scalded
2 tablespoons sugar
¼ cup shortening (butter, margarine, oil)

2½ teaspoons salt
7 cups all-purpose flour (try
your flour variations)

For Spread:
1 egg, beaten
½ cup shortening, melted

Dissolve yeast in warm water, using your large mixing bowl. Set aside while you mix milk, salt, sugar, and shortening in another bowl. Spoon milk mixture into yeast-water mixture; stir. Slowly add flour as needed. Mix well until dough is smooth and satiny. Turn out onto lightly floured board; knead for 12 minutes. Place in greased bowl. Cover with clean cloth, place in warm place for 45 minutes until double in bulk.

Punch dough down and turn out on lightly floured board once more. Let the dough rest while you grease 2 bread pans 9 by 5 by 3 inches. Cut dough in half, and roll into balls, then shape into rectangles ¼ to ½ inch thick (the length of the pan).

Brush with melted shortening (butter or margarine), und der beaten egg. Spread the desired filling over the rectangles, roll jelly-roll fashion, seal edges, and place edge down in pans. Brush tops with melted shortening and cover with clean cloth. Let rise for nearly 1 hour. Bake in a 400° F. oven for 1 hour. Turn out on racks to cool, or serve warm.

"Thinking is like loving and dying—each of us must do it for himself."—JOSIAH ROYCE

Filling Variations

(Mutter's Own Fillings and Sauces)

Sorry, do not have measurements of ingredients, as Mother cooked and baked fillings, sauces, and jellies-preserves by faith alone.

ANCHOVY-CAPER FILLING. Boil anchovy fillets, crushed capers, lemon slices, minced cloves of garlic, chopped parsley, dry white wine, whipped butter. For a sauce add consommé and gravy.

ANCHOVY SPREAD. Mash and mix anchovy fillets, tomato paste, and minced garlic cloves; beat with egg, cayenne pepper, and paprika.

HERBED BUTTER SPREAD. Mix well butter, orégano, basil, minced parsley, and garlic.

CINNAMON-BUTTER SPREAD. Mix butter, cinnamon, and sugar.

PRUNE-APPLE SPREAD. Boil prunes, apples, and touches of sugar, cinnamon, and lemon juice.

HERB FILLING. Chopped scallions, chopped parsley, minced garlic cloves, and butter. Cook till not quite browned; then add beaten egg, salt, Tabasco sauce, and black pepper to taste, mixing well.

DATE-NUT FILLING. Mix chopped dates, chopped nuts (your favorites), and grated lemon rind.

CRANBERRY FILLING. Cook cranberries and sugar over low heat until cranberries pop open.

RAISIN-FRUIT FILLING. Mix raisins (or currants), chopped candied fruit (citron and cherries), cinnamon, butter, and sugar.

There are many others, but these are the ones I remember from teen-age days.

"To know how sweet your home may be, just go away—but keep the key."

Father's Tannenbaum Brot

This holiday recipe of my father's, plus many others, was treasured highly by Dad, for as a boy learning the baking trade, he baked and sold this fine mix ("undt der stollen midt from der mix") on the streets of Hamburg, Germany.

2 packages active dry yeast (or starter)
½ cup warm water
2 teaspoons salt
2 cups lukewarm milk

½ cup sugar
2 eggs
½ cup soft shortening
8 cups all-purpose flour (or a blend)

Dissolve yeast in warm water in large bowl; let rest for a moment. Stir and mix in salt, sugar, and milk. Add shortening, eggs, and half the flour; then hand-mix, preferably (see Variations* on pp. 115–16) while you add the rest of flour. Turn out on lightly floured board and knead for nearly five minutes until satiny-smooth. Place in a greased bowl, turn once, cover with a damp cloth, and let rise in warm place until doubled in bulk (90 minutes). Punch down, let rise again for ½ hour,† then cut dough for size of pans. Shape dough, place in greased pans, cover again, let rise in warm place for 15 minutes. Bake in 375° F. oven for three-quarters of an hour.

Variations

As this is a basic yeast dough, all sorts of marvels can be created from the above, and as Mother and her mother turned out dozens of little tantalizers from leftover dough, you can too! "Der eggzamples, pbleze, Johann, ja?"

† At this point take ½ of the dough and roll dough ⅓-inch thick; then cut with sharp knife or cutter into diamonds or rectangles and spread fruit preserves on dough. Then roll up angles (corners) to cover preserves. Place these sweet rolls on greased cookie pan or cake pan. Brush with melted butter or margarine, cover with a clean cloth, let rise in warm place until almost doubled. Oven at 350° F. for ½ hour will do nicely; "spatula" rolls to rack to cool a bit, then glaze tops.

* A perfect Fröhliche Weihnachten is always said with a stollen under each arm. At point (*) of our Tannenbaum mix, cut dough and use half for kneading-in ½ cup chopped almonds, ¼ cup each of cut-up citron and candied cherries, 1 cup seedless raisins, and 1 tablespoon grated lemon peel. (Please do not grate the white.) Roll out dough into an oval shape, 9 by 12 inches; den mit der szoft butter spread. Fold the edge nearest you (long way) up over to the edge away from you, press edges down firmly. Place on greased pan or sheet, brush top with melted butter, cover, and let rise until double (a little over ½ hour). Bake in 375° F. oven for ½ hour or until a golden brown; frost and enjoy.

The wonderful breads and kaffee kuchen never lasted long on Grossmutter's wood-burning range when the Rahns togedder got. Do you remember the large warmer above the range?— you are as young as you feel, you know!

* TANNENBAUM FRUIT BREAD. Please follow the Tannenbaum Brot recipe, except at point *, instead of rest of flour, add ¼ teaspoon nutmeg, ¼ teaspoon mace, ⅛ teaspoon cloves, ¼ cup raisins, ¼ cup cut-up candied cherries, 2 tablespoons chopped nuts, 2 tablespoons chopped citron. Then follow Tannenbaum recipe.

* ANOTHER SCHLESWIG-HOLSTEIN VARIATION. Please follow the Tannenbaum Brot recipe, except at point *, instead of rest of flour, add ¼ cup diced candied fruit, ¼ cup seedless raisins, ¼ cup chopped nuts, ¼ teaspoon anise, ¼ teaspoon vanilla. Continue with Tannenbaum recipe. What a gracious holiday gift!

Here is Abigail Van Buren's "Recipe for Happiness." This most unusual and enthusiastic person has helped thousands of people along the old daily road; read her column.

Take 2 heaping cups of patience, 1 heartful of love, 2 handfuls of generosity, a dash of laughter, 1 headful of understanding. Sprinkle generously with kindness, add plenty of faith, and mix well; spread over a period of a lifetime and serve everybody you meet!

"The best teacher one can have is necessity."

—FRANÇOIS DE LA NOUS

Braué's Fröhliche Weihnachten Brot
Merry Christmas Bread

2 packages active dry yeast
¼ cup warm water
2½ teaspoons salt
½ cup melted butter (margarine)
½ cup sugar
1 cup milk, scalded
2 eggs, beaten
2 teaspoons grated lemon peel
¼ teaspoon almond extract
6 cups sifted all-purpose flour (or unbleached)

Dissolve and stir yeast in water in small bowl. Let stand 12 minutes while you stir butter, salt, and sugar in a large mixing bowl; top it with milk and stir until mixed. Let stand until lukewarm, then stir in half the flour and the yeast mixture; blend until smooth. Beat in eggs, almond extract, and lemon peel along with rest of flour to make a soft, doughy mixture.

Turn out dough onto a lightly floured board; knead for 10 minutes. Place in greased bowl in ball shape, turn over once in bowl, cover with clean cloth. Let stand in warm place (home at Christmastide!) nearly 2 hours. During this anticipating interim, mix together—

4 tablespoons syrup (corn or
your favorite)
½ cup brown sugar, packed

½ cup butter, melted
2 teaspoons water, not cold

Put this mixture in bottom of greased loaf pans, then mix in a bowl—

1 cup brown sugar, packed
and set aside until ready for
dough

1½ cups of seedless raisins
1 teaspoon ground cinnamon
2 tablespoons butter, melted

Punch down dough and turn out onto lightly floured board. Divide into equal portions, roll out into 12-by-9-inch rectangles, spread with raisin mixture.

Now, from the shorter side (end), roll dough tightly. (Duplicate with other rectangle.) Cut rolls into one-inch slices, place in pans, cover with waxed paper and clean cloth. Let rise in a warm place for an hour; bake in a 350° F. oven for a bit over 45 minutes; turn out of pans, and serve!

Braué's Basic Sweet Dough

Party inspirations.

3 packages active dry yeast
1 cup warm water
1 cup sugar
1 cup milk, scalded

1¼ teaspoons salt
6 tablespoons shortening
3 eggs, beaten
7 cups all-purpose flour

Dissolve the yeast in the warm water and sprinkle in 3 tablespoons sugar. Set aside while in another bowl you combine the milk, the rest of the sugar, salt, and shortening. Add this milk mixture to the yeast mixture and add the eggs and half the flour, stirring until nice and smooth, then stir in the rest of the flour until it is pliable.

Turn out on a lightly floured board, knead for at least 5 minutes. Place in a greased bowl and turn the dough over once so that it will all be greased.

Cover and let rise in a warm place for almost an hour and then proceed with any of the following desired variations.

Braué's Sweet Dough Pan Bread

Topping optional.

Punch down the sweet dough when double in bulk and divide into equal portions. Roll each piece into a circle about ¼ inch thick. The size is determined by your cake pans. Place dough in greased cake pans, cover, and let rise in a warm place until doubled in bulk. Press a ¼ cup of raisins into dough an inch or two apart. Bake in a 375° F. oven for 10 minutes. Then pour the syrup or topping over the top of the cake while in the oven and continue baking for 30 minutes longer. Remove from pan for serving or storing.

Syrup Topping for Sweet Rolls

Stir and mix in a saucepan 3 tablespoons butter, 3 tablespoons water (variable), ⅔ cup sugar, ¼ cup of brown sugar. Boil over low heat for at least 5 minutes.

Sweet Dough Cut-ups

Punch sweet dough down when doubled in bulk, turn out on a lightly floured board.

Divide into 3 equal pieces and roll each piece out on to an oblong of 14 by 9 inches. Brush lightly with melted butter (or margarine or oil), then sprinkle with a blend of 2 cups sugar, 1 tablespoon cinnamon, 1 cup seedless raisins.

Sprinkle ⅓ of this mixture on each oblong of sweet dough; roll each piece up lengthwise like a jelly roll. Cut with a sharp knife into slices about ½ inch thick.

Place cut sides up about an inch apart on a greased shallow baking pan. Cover and let rise in a warm place until doubled in bulk. Bake in a 425° F. oven for about 20 minutes.

Ice the tops while still warm with this plain homemade icing if desired: Combine and beat until smooth ½ cup of confectioners' sugar, 2 teaspoons milk, ⅛ teaspoon vanilla extract.

Dad's Hot Cross Buns

Dad, as a boy apprentice, baked and sold these traditional Lenten "one a penny, two a penny" buns.

2 packages active dry yeast (or starter)
½ cup warm water
1 teaspoon salt
1 cup milk, scalded and cooled to lukewarm
¼ cup sugar
¼ cup shortening (or oil)

1 egg, beaten well
½ cup seedless raisins
½ teaspoon cinnamon
½ teaspoon nutmeg
6 cups sifted all-purpose flour (or a blend)
"glug" of milk for brushing rolls
confectioners' frosting

Dissolve yeast in water in large bowl. Stir in milk, shortening, salt, and sugar; then stir in egg, cinnamon, nutmeg, raisins, and half the flour, mixing well. Blend in rest of flour to make a soft, satiny dough; stir until dough pulls away from sides of bowl.

Turn out dough onto lightly floured board, knead well until elastic. Place dough in large greased bowl, then up-end dough so bottom is top. Cover with a clean cloth; let rise in warm place for 30 minutes (until doubled in bulk).

Punch down dough, turn out onto lightly floured board, cut into equal sizes. Shape into balls and place in greased baking dishes or cookie pans. Cover and let rise once more until doubled in bulk (30 minutes). Brush tops lightly with milk and bake in 375° F. oven for 30 minutes or until golden brown. Remove from dishes or pan and cross tops with confectioners' frosting. Ideal for teatime or kaffee.

What has happened to the "thunderingly stirring" recounts of our own family history and our great nation's heritage? Are we that busy with our lives of tension?

"The art of silence is as great as that of speech."
                                        —Old Deutsche words

Braué's Norwegian Holiday Bread

Julekake—a great favorite with Norwegians, with or without butter, with morning and afternoon coffee.

1 package active dry yeast
½ cup warm water
½ cup milk, scalded
½ cup butter, melted
¼ cup granulated sugar
1 teaspoon salt
1 egg, beaten
1 cup seedless raisins
1 teaspoon powdered cardamom

¼ cup chopped orange peel
¼ cup chopped pineapple
¼ cup chopped candied
   cherries (optional)
4 cups sifted all-purpose flour
1 egg white, beaten
confectioners' glaze
candied cherries (topping)
angelica leaves (topping)

Dissolve yeast in warm water in a large bowl. Stir in milk and butter (lukewarm); then stir in salt, sugar, egg, raisins, cardamom, orange peel, pineapple, and cherries, stirring, stirring. Gradually stir in flour; beat until dough is stiff. Cover with a clean cloth, place in warm place, and let rise for 2 hours.

Turn dough onto a lightly floured board and knead lightly until, all of a sudden, no stickiness! Cut dough in half, shape into balls, place into two greased coffee cans; cover with a clean cloth and let rise in a warm place for nearly an hour.

Brush with egg white and bake in 350° F. oven for nearly 40 minutes. Remove from cans, cool on rack, glaze and decorate with cherries and leaves!

"Justifying a fault doubles it."—French saying

Rahn-Braué Brioches

A continental breakfast since baking began.

1 package active dry yeast
¼ cup warm water
½ teaspoon salt
1 tablespoon sugar
1 tablespoon cream

3 eggs beaten with 1 yolk (set
   aside 1 egg white)
1 cup soft butter
3 cups all-purpose flour

The night before baking, dissolve yeast in water in a large bowl. Add sugar, salt, cream, and butter; add eggs and yolk; mix well. Add flour; beat until satiny-smooth; cover with a clean cloth and place in refrigerator while you sleep, dreaming of sweet rolls.

In the morning (let daughter try), remove dough and turn out on a lightly floured board; cut and shape three-quarters of dough into 1½- to 2-inch balls. Shape rest of dough into 1- to 1¼-inch balls. Place larger balls in bottom of greased muffin pans; press a dent in each with thumb and place smaller balls in dent.

Brush surface of balls with egg white (or melted butter), cover with a clean cloth, and let rise for a little over an hour. Bake in a 375° F. oven for 20 minutes.

"No one can give you better advice than yourself."—CICERO

Dad's Basic Italian Bread

A spectacular favorite of all churches—an ecumenical pioneer.

1 package active dry yeast (or 2 cups starter) dissolved in
1 cup warm water
2 teaspoons salt (might need a bit more)
4 cups all-purpose flour (or a blend of flours)

Mix 1 cup flour with yeast mixture. Turn out on a lightly floured board. Knead until smooth. Turn soft dough out in a floured mixing bowl, cover with a damp towel, and let rise for 2 hours.

Mix the remainder of flour in water until smooth. Turn out on a lightly floured board and add to the soft-dough mixture. Knead until dough is satin-smooth. Turn dough out on a large floured board, cover, and let rise for 4 hours. Now, Johann, knead yust vunsz moah!

Shape into a round or long loaf, place on a greased baking sheet (or earthenware). Brush top with olive oil (or nutritional oil). Cover with clean cloth, let rise a bit, and bake in a 450° F. oven for 40 minutes.

Dad's Italian Pizza Dough

1 package active dry yeast (or 2 cups starter), dissolved in
1 cup warm water
1 egg yolk, beaten
½ teaspoon salt, blended with 2 cups all-purpose flour (or a blend of flours with unbleached white)

Mix all ingredients together with a fork, gradually adding the flour. Turn out dough on a lightly floured board and knead until smooth. Turn dough into a flour-sprinkled bowl. Cover with a damp cloth and let rise for 2 hours in a warm place, until doubled in bulk (a dry towel will form a hard crust). Use the dough with your favorite pizza recipe.

"What is thought without a double strength of wisdom?"
—MILTON

Dad's Original Torino Bread Sticks

Dad exchanged recipes with the Italianos in the Italian Alps—the pumpernickel bread and rye bread for the bread stick and pizza-dough recipes.

1 package active dry yeast (or 2 cups starter), dissolved in
1 cup warm water
¼ cup milk, warm
3 tablespoons butter (or oil)
1 teaspoon salt
1 teaspoon sugar, blended with
3 cups all-purpose flour (or a blend of flours)

Incorporate yeast mixture with 1 cup flour in a mixing bowl. Turn out on a lightly floured board and knead until smooth. Place the dough in a floured bowl. Cover with a damp cloth, and let rise for at least 3 hours.

Mix the rest of the ingredients together into a smooth dough and turn out on a lightly floured board, then add the risen dough to the smooth dough and knead until satin-smooth. Spoon dough into a large floured bowl; cover and let stand until doubled in bulk.

Turn out the dough to the lightly floured board and knead

until it is elastic and does not stick to board. Slice the dough into equal pieces (about 24). Shape each piece by rolling the dough between hands and board until it looks like a short rope. Place on oiled or greased baking sheet (or earthenware) about an inch apart. Brush with milk.

Bake at 450° F. for 5 to 10 minutes or until crispy golden. A crisp comrade with barbecue, cheese, soups and stews!

"MEDICAL PROGRESS: *In days of old, the ancestors were revered on the wall, now in the flesh.*"

Starter Dough

Make the starter dough with ½ the recipe ingredients on p. 124, except the yeast (use 1 package). After all blending has been accomplished, cover with a clean cloth and let stand in a warm place for overnight souring (at least 12 hours). Starter may be kept in freezer for a month (carefully covered), and may be used from the refrigerator for a week: remember it must be warmed to room temperature.

"The world is like a rose garden—plenty of thorns and black spots, but there are roses."—A Rosarian

Another point to consider on "the old days" versus "the modern days" is that though the times are different and present-day mixes may be better (absurd! I disclaim this!), modern cakes and breads lose prestige and character, for the honor goes to a mammoth concern, not to the individual. The modern housewife has had her life mechanized and simplified into "quick mixes" until the pride of artistic accomplishment is gone. Art is a definite part of the word "artisan."

"Bread is the staff of man's existence.
Bread is wheat and wheat is earth, the good earth,
The black earth out of which comes man's food,
His health, his vigor, his long life . . ."
—LOUIS BROMFIELD

Dad's Alsatian Sour-Dough French Bread

Dad brought a jar of this starter dough with him when he came to the United States.

Mother and Dad had grown up as friends in the beautiful old village of Suderstapel in Schleswig-Holstein, and when Grossmutter brought the nine Rahn children to the United States in steerage, Dad could not remain behind without Mother, and he followed soon after. They were married in Omaha and moved to Council Bluffs, Iowa, to go into the bread-baking business.

1 package active dry yeast (or 2 cups sour-dough starter), dissolved in
¼ cup warm water
2½ teaspoons salt
4½ teaspoons sugar
½ cup milk

1 cup water
1½ tablespoons shortening or salad oil
6 cups sifted all-purpose flour (or unbleached)
2 tablespoons starter dough

Add sugar and salt to yeast (starter) mixture. Let rest while you pan-boil water, oil, and milk; cool to lukewarm (98° F.). Pour milk mixture into yeast mixture, stirring constantly. Pour a little over 4 cups of flour into mixture, blending well; add the starter, stir, stir, and stir. Do not fret; dough will be soft. Place in greased bowl, cover with a clean cloth, and let stand in a warm place until doubled in size.

Turn onto lightly floured board; no kneading; cut in half with sharp knife or cutter; flatten halves with hands. Mold as if making loaves, then roll into long, tapered loaves 16 to 18 inches long and about 2 inches high. Place on baking sheet sprinkled with flour, oatmeal, or oil. Gash, with a sharp knife, nearly 2 inches apart, diagonal cuts in loaves (¼ inch deep). Let rise again until doubled in size and bake in a 430° F. oven for 15 minutes; then reduce oven to 345° F. and bake 20 minutes longer.

Brush tops and sides with egg white or butter, or sprinkle with flour (another desired way) and bake for 5 more minutes. Cool on rack.

Braué's Crusty French Bread

From the romantic family branches of the Rahns and Braués—a delight with thick soups and heady cheeses!

1 package active dry yeast
3 cups warm water (110° F.)
1 tablespoon sugar
1 tablespoon salt
6 cups all-purpose flour (or yedt beddter, unbleached)

2 tablespoons soft shortening
corn meal (a bit)
½ cup water
½ teaspoon salt
1½ teaspoons cornstarch
sesame seeds

Combine yeast, warm water, sugar, add 1 tablespoon salt with enough stirring to dissolve yeast; let stand 5 minutes. Stir in flour and shortening; then work flour in with hands. Knead until smooth and elastic (on floured board, if I forget to mention). Cover with a clean tea towel; let rise in warm place until doubled in size.

Shape into three or four balls. Let dough rest 15 minutes. Shape each ball into a roll 12 to 15 inches long, tapered like a boat at each end. Place on a baking sheet or pan sprinkled, in a Presbyterian manner, with corn meal. Cover with towel; let rise not quite 60 minutes—to keep you interested.

In the interim, combine remaining water, salt, cornstarch. Cook and stir until clear but thick. Brush over loaves (on all brushing duties, please use pastry brush similar to paintbrush); sprinkle tops of loaves with sesame seed. With sharp knife, gash, diagonally, 3 to 4 stripes in each loaf, ½ to ¼ inch deep; this is when you will possess the feeling of victory or defeat, breadwise!

Heat oven to 425°–450° F. Place a large pan of hot water on lower shelf of oven. Move your luscious loaves on upper shelf. Bake 5 to 10 minutes; reduce heat to moderate (325°–350° F.) and bake 50 to 60 minutes longer.

These will be three or four of the most delicious loaves you have ever exclaimed over—you will want it often with crisp-cool salads too!

"The hurrier I go, the behinder I get!"—Penn Dutch saying

Braué's Normandy French Bread

A la customer from Canada, passing through Council Bluffs en route to New Orleans.

1 package or cake of yeast (or 2 cups starter)
2 cups water, warm
1 tablespoon sugar
2 teaspoons salt
6 cups all-purpose flour
1 egg white, unbeaten

Dissolve yeast in water; add sugar, salt, and about 3 cups of flour. Beat until shiny smooth. Stir in about 2 more cups flour. (Dad used to counsel me that, in this work, "about" is a most exact word after many bakings.) Knead on floured board until satiny-smooth. Let dough rise in greased bowl until doubled in bulk (almost 1 hour). If you are so fortunate as to possess a wooden batch box or crock, so much the better!

Punch down, cut into desired sizes, and shape into balls. Let dough rest 5 or 6 minutes. Rub a little corn oil or shortening on your hands and roll each ball between hands to form long, slender loaves, making the ends smaller. Place loaves on baking sheet or pan sprinkled with flour or corn meal, or greased. Cut diagonal gashes in loaves (½ to ¾ inch deep, couple of inches apart on top of loaves), cover with cloth, and let rise 60 minutes.

Bake in hot oven, 425°–450° F., for 35 minutes. Remove from oven, brush with egg white, and return to oven for 2 or 3 minutes. Remove and place on cooling rack, with a call to family and friends to come and sample as is or with any good food!

Rahn-Braué's Sour-Dough French Bread

Le Boulanger's bread.

1 cup starter
1 cup lukewarm water
1 tablespoon shortening, soft, melted (or oil, butter, etc.)
1½ teaspoons salt
4 cups all-purpose flour (or unbleached flour) plus
a pinch of soda

In a large mixing bowl combine first four ingredients. Stir this mixture until it is dissolved and completely blended. Add the flour and mix well. Turn out and place on a lightly floured board. Turn the dough over several times until it handles easily and is elastically smooth. Place in a greased bowl, cover with a clean cloth, and let rise in warm place for 2 hours.

Punch the dough down and knead for about 20 times, until all the air is removed from the dough. (Use a rolling pin and press out the air.) Now roll the dough into an oblong shape, preferably 12 by 16 inches or 9 by 14 inches. Take the long side and "jelly-roll" the dough, sealing the edges. Seal very well and gently stretch the bread into a desired length.

Place on a greased baking sheet, tin or earthenware. Sprinkle with corn meal or bran. Brush the top of the loaf with water and slash it diagonally in several places. Again let rise for about 90 minutes in a warm place. Bake in a 450° F. oven for at least 10 minutes; then lower the temperature to 375° F. and bake for 20 more minutes. The bread should be a golden brown. Remove from oven to cooling rack.

Sour-Dough Starter

Now a good starter for this sour-dough bread, the starter that Mother and Dad brought over from the old country in jars. The ingredients you will need are—

6 good potatoes
2 quarts boiling water
¼ cup sugar
3 tablespoons salt
1 cup lukewarm water

1 cake of compressed yeast—
unless you have farmer's
yeast, Uncle John's yeast, or
bakers' yeast

Be sure you cook the potatoes in boiling water until they are very tender. Drain and save the water. Set the potatoes aside to be mashed (or purée the potatoes if you wish). Dissolve the yeast in the lukewarm water. Mash the potatoes; add them to the remaining ingredients, including the potato water. Stir until creamy and place in a large bowl or crock. Cover and place in a warm spot to ferment for about 48 hours. Then store in a cold place in jars and use as needed.

Phoebe's Wiebke-Rahn French Bread

Our Alsatian relations' recipe for our quick-mix friends.

1 package active dry yeast
3 cups warm water (variable)
a bit of shortening
1 tablespoon salt
2 tablespoons sugar

1 cup corn meal, or bran
½ cup sesame seeds (optional)
6 cups all-purpose flour (unbleached and white)

Dissolve yeast in warm water in large mixing bowl. Stir in sugar and salt, plus half the flour, until smooth. Gradually add the remainder of flour, until dough is stiff. Turn out onto lightly floured board, knead until dough is smooth and elastic, adding enough flour to prevent stickiness.

Place in lightly greased bowl, turn over once, cover with a clean cloth, place in warm place, and let rise for an hour. Punch dough down; let rise until doubled in bulk. Turn out onto lightly floured board, shape into ball, cut in half or thirds, and mold into boat-shaped loaves. Be sure the ends are sealed.

Place on greased, corn-meal(or bran)-sprinkled sheets (or earthenware, or foil shaped into boats). Diagonally cut tops with a sharp knife, brush with water, sprinkle with sesame seeds. Cover with a clean cloth; let rise in a warm place for 30 minutes. Bake in moist 375° F. oven for 50 minutes (or 450° F. for 10 minutes, then 350° for 30 minutes). Cool on rack.

"Yesterday is a canceled check, tomorrow is a promissory note, today is ready cash."—my parents' banker, the good HUBERT TINLEY

RYE BREADS

Rye flour is a low-gluten flour that possesses a delicate cell structure. Most American rye-bread recipes call for wheat flour or white flour to make a light, porous, less-crumbly loaf. The liquid in the dough mixture holds the leavening gas, producing the porousness. Rye bread baked with all-rye flour will be heavier and more compact. The rye dough will not rise as well as the wheat-flour mix, and once it has risen it is hard to keep it up. Warm the rye flour; make sure that the yeast is fresh and is dissolved in liquid at the right temperature, and that there is enough flour to make a pliable, workable dough. For heavy and sticky 'twill be otherwise.

Do not sift rye flour and do not let rye dough rise too long (but it must rise longer than dough for white bread). Humid heat is the best for rye-bread and dark-dough risings. The second rising before the dough is shaped into loaves should be of the same warmth, 80° to 85° F.

All milk, whether it be sweet, buttermilk, or sour, should be scalded in making of dark and rye breads to produce the fine grain and texture, the velvet touch. Buttermilk, sour milk, and cream will curdle when heated, but it will not harm the bread.

Baking bread in a humid oven produces a thick, crispy crust. For glistening crusts, brush tops with cold water, milk, or beer. Caraway, orange peel, anise, are good flavors with rye bread, as are variations: sugar, molasses, honey, and sorghum.

My father used to bake the full-flavored rye breads on the oven tiles, and our families of long ago bake-cooked in and on earthenware. Try a batch on a slab of baked terra-cotta, glazed clay, a clay bowl, tile. Ask for a Mexican bread plate one day, and watch the Spanish eyes light up. Sprinkle ware with bran, corn meal, or your favorite flour before baking. You might need a bakers' peel (flat wooden shovel).

Yeast bread rises faster at high altitudes. Always check the dough 15 minutes sooner than ordinary before molding into loaves and baking. When at high altitude, be sure to check with your university and utility companies for the correct baking and mixing procedures.

"The punishment of wise men who refuse to take part in the affairs of government is to live under the government of unwise men."—PLATO

Braué's Modern Rye-Wheat Bread

A most attractive loaf, eye-appealing and taste-wise.

2 packages active dry yeast (or 2 cups starter)
3 cups milk, scalded (always cool to lukewarm, which is actually cooler to the touch than body temperature)
3 tablespoons honey (or syrup)
3 tablespoons nutritional oil (or your choice)
1 tablespoon salt
½ cup nutritional yeast (optional)
4 cups rye flour, blended with
4 cups whole-wheat flour (or a stone-ground flour blend)

Dissolve yeast in milk in a large mixing bowl. Set aside, and in another bowl mix one cup of flour and all the other ingredients. Mix thoroughly. Then add this mixture to the yeast mixture and continue to add more of the flour, making the dough the right consistency for kneading. Knead until stiff but pliable, and place in a greased bowl. Turn the dough over once, cover with a damp cloth, and set in a warm place to rise until doubled in bulk.

Punch the dough down and let rise again. Turn out on a lightly floured board and knead for just a few moments. Then divide and shape into loaves of equal size. (This is where a scale comes in handy.) Place in greased bread pans. Cover with damp cloth, let rise until light, and bake in a 320° F. oven for at least 90 minutes.

Backermeister Christian Friedrich Braué's Russian Rye

One of many of the successful and winning dark breads baked by Johann Braué and Christian Braué, brothers. This was baked by Uncle Christian, under trying conditions as a Russian prisoner, for the Czar's troops.

First Saur Sponge:

2 cups starter, or	1 cup water, warm
sponge left from last baking	2 cups rye meal

Mix to fairly stiff dough. Cover, and let stand in a warm place for 4 hours.

Second Sponge:
1 cup water, warm
2 cups rye flour

Mix and add to first sponge. Cover, and let rise for 4 hours.

Third Sponge:
2 cups water, warm
1 package active dry yeast (or homemade yeast)
3 cups rye flour

Dissolve yeast in water. Gradually add flour, and mix until smooth. Add to two-stage sponge and incorporate well. Cover and let stand until dough drops (2 hours).

Fourth Sponge:	1 teaspoon caraway seeds,
water, warm (variable)	ground (optional)
2 teaspoons salt	2 cups unbleached flour
1 tablespoon malt	

Mix all ingredients well and add to three-stage sponge. Mix until first appearance of smoothness. Turn out onto a lightly floured board, cover, and let rest for a few moments. Knead; make up into round or long loaves. Place on corn-meal-dusted baking sheets or earthenware. Cover; let rise for 1 hour. Dock a few times, and bake in a 375° F. oven for 60 to 75 minutes.

"Never ask pardon before you are accused."

My Father's Norwegian Rye Bread

Army fare of all Nordics.

1 package yeast, dissolved in
1 cup warm water (or 2 cups
 starter)
1 cup milk, scalded (or stock)
1 tablespoon sugar (or honey)
1 tablespoon salt

3 medium potatoes, boiled and
 mashed
1 cup molasses
2 cups rye flour
2 cups graham flour

The flours should be blended before mixing; incorporate the flour, salt and sugar. (If honey is used, add it to the molasses.) Make a well in the dry mixture, and pour and stir in as much milk as the dry ingredients will absorb, making a stiff batter. Then add mashed potatoes and molasses. Stir well and add the dissolved yeast mixture or starter. Cover and let stand overnight in a warm place.

Then, in the good morning, add a cup of milk and water and enough white flour to give it good consistency. Cover and let stand until doubled in bulk. Turn out on a floured board and shape into loaves. Place in greased bread pans and let rise a bit, then bake in a 350° F. oven for an hour.

"There is no time like the present."—SMOLLETT

Dad's Hundred-Per-Cent Rye Bread

Rye flour is a lively substitute for wheat flour when the person is allergic to wheat. Try it in sour and steam mixes.

1 package active dry yeast (or 2 cups starter or homemade yeast)
2 cups milk, scalded (or stock or potato water)
2 tablespoons molasses (or honey or sorghum)
1 egg, beaten
1 tablespoon salt
½ cup nutritional yeast (or brewers' yeast; optional)
2 tablespoons caraway seeds, whole (or anise seeds), optional
8 cups rye flour (variable)

Dissolve the yeast in the milk in a large mixing bowl. Add and blend in molasses and egg. Add half the rye flour and all the other ingredients and mix well until smooth. Cover and let stand in warm place for at least half an hour.

Blend in the remaining rye flour and mix well. Cover again and let stand again for 30 minutes. Stir down the dough to make sure that it is of good consistency.

Turn out onto a lightly floured board. Knead well. Divide in half, mold into loaves, and place into bread pans. (Or mold into long or round loaves and place on greased earthenware or baking tins.) Cover and let stand until the dough has doubled in size.

Bake at 350° F. for an hour. Turn out onto racks to cool.

"Happiness is not a goal; it's a way of living."

Braué's Amerikaner-Deutsche Schwarzbrot

A dark bread of most loyal German-American heritage.

2 cups starter (2 packages dry yeast)
1 quart potato water, warm (or stock)
2 cups potatoes, puréed (or instant potatoes)
1 tablespoon salt
½ cup nutritional yeast (optional)
1 tablespoon caraway seeds, whole (optional)
8 cups rye flour, blended thoroughly with
4 cups whole-wheat flour (or a blend of flours)

Dissolve yeast in warm potato water in large mixing bowl. Add and stir in other ingredients, gradually stirring in the flour. Blend well and turn out onto lightly floured board. Knead until smooth and pliable. Place in greased bowl, turn dough over once, and let rise until doubled.

Turn out onto floured board, divide dough evenly, shape into long or round loaves, and place on greased baking sheets (or earthenware). Cover and let rise until doubled in size. Bake in 380° oven for nearly an hour. Turn out to cooling racks and brush tops with a touch bit of oil or water.

Dad's Swiss-German Rye Bread

A most helpful contribution from the German-Swiss border.

2 packages active dry yeast (or 2 cups starter)
3 cups potato water, warm
1 tablespoon salt
2 tablespoons molasses (or syrup, honey)
½ cup nutritional yeast (or brewers' yeast), optional
8 cups rye flour (or a blend of dark flours)

Dissolve the yeast in half of the potato water. Let stand until bubbly. Add the remaining potato water, half the flour, then the rest of the ingredients. Mix well. Cover and let stand in a fairly cool place or at room temperature for at least a day (24 hours or a little longer).

Then add the remaining flour, or enough to make dough elastically smooth. Turn out on a lightly floured board and knead for 10 or 12 minutes. Place in an oiled or greased bowl. Turn the dough over once, cover, and let rise in a warm place until doubled in bulk. This will take 4 to 5 hours.

Turn out on a lightly floured board. Divide the dough equally and shape into round loaves. Oil the dough and place on baking sheets or earthenware. Let dough rest for few moments until it has risen slightly and spread out a bit. Bake in a 300° F. oven for at least an hour. It might take a little longer than an hour, but 'tis worth it.

Dad's Graham-Rye Bread

1930's—the great depression. Mother and Dad built a garage with this great recipe by bartering with a carpenter-builder who had a large family!

1 package dry yeast (or 2 cups starter or home yeast)
1 tablespoon salt
⅓ cup molasses
3 tablespoons melted butter or lard

1 cup milk
3 cups warm water
2 cups graham-rye flour (another chance for dark-flour blending)
7 cups all-purpose flour

Dissolve yeast in a large bowl with 1 cup warm water; let stand for a few moments. Add just enough all-purpose flour to make a light, soft sponge (starter), and beat well. Cover with a clean cloth and let rest for the space of time to prepare in another bowl: To 2 cups warm water add molasses, butter or lard, salt, and graham-rye flour, stirring well. Add this mixture to yeast sponge, beating until smooth.

Without stopping, add 5 cups of all-purpose flour, and make a dough that handles easily. Lightly knead dough on a floured board until satiny-smooth.

Place in greased bowl, cover with cloth, and set in warm place. Let rise until double in bulk (90 minutes). Cut into portions, shape into loaves, and place in your now favorite bread pans, cover again and let rise for an hour. Bake in 375° F. oven for 50 minutes. A nutty, flavorful loaf.

"Mit Deutsche brot, wunderbar rye, der is szo Genucht dot meets der eye."

Rahn's Der Saxon Rye Brick Bread

A heavy, healthful loaf—slice thin for true tastiness.

4 cups water, boiling
1½ teaspoons salt
2 tablespoons honey
2 tablespoons butter
¼ cup bran (or flaxseed meal, or wheat germ)

1 cup wheat grits (or your favorite grits)
4 cups rye meal (pumpernickel rye)
some corn meal

Mix all ingredients except corn meal together in a large mixing bowl. Cover, let stand overnight at room temperature.

In der morgen, shape into loaf and roll in corn meal (bran, flaxseed meal, or wheat germ). Bake in 200° F. oven, in covered pan, moist from pan of hot water in oven, for 4 hours.

Cool on rack, though I'm sure you will be tasting by slicing off thin tasties (spread with butter or cheese spread). To save, wrap in tea towel and place in refrigerator—yes, ma'am—reheat!

"A man is not better than his conversation."—German saying

Dad's Pottawattamie County Rye Bread

The pride of the county!

1 package active dry yeast
2 cups warm water (112° F.)
2 teaspoons salt
3 cups unbleached flour
2 cups rye flour (blend flours well)

2 tablespoons soft shortening (lard)
2 tablespoons brown sugar
1 teaspoon caraway seeds, if desired

Dissolve yeast in warm water in large mixing bowl. Add to yeast mixture half the flour plus all the brown sugar, salt, shortening, and caraway seeds. (All families do not relish caraway seeds.) As you mix by hand or spoon (or mixer at half speed), stir in remaining flour vigorously. Turn over twice in large greased bowl, and cover with a clean cloth. Let rise in a warm place until double in size.

Stir a bit for luck, as long as a 30-second commercial; cut up and shape into loaves, using greased pan or bread pans. Lovingly pat top of loaves with floured hands and bake in a preheated 375° F. oven until golden brown, or 50 minutes. Brush with shortening, cool, and serve.

This was another one of Dad's outstanding depression days barter-batters!

"Nobody calls himself a rogue."

Braué's Nordic Rye Bread

A real favorite with the Iowa farmer!

2 packages active dry yeast (home yeast, or starter)
2 cups warm water
¼ cup molasses (this may be too rich for some, zo oudt der molasses leave)
½ cup sugar

1 tablespoon salt
finely grated rind of 1 or 2 oranges
2 tablespoons soft shortening (dietetic oil, or your choice)
3 cups rye flour
3 cups sifted all-purpose flour

Dissolve yeast in water in large mixing bowl. Stir in sugar, salt, molasses, and orange rind. Add the shortening and half the flour mixture (first blend and reblend the flours in large bowl), and mix with large spoon. Add rest of flour mixture and mix with hands.

Turn onto lightly floured board, and knead well until satiny-smooth. Round up in greased bowl, making sure all dough is lightly greased. Cover with a damp cloth, and let rise in a warm place for about 2 hours, until double in bulk.

Punch down; round up again; re-cover and let rise, about 45 minutes this time. Punch down with anticipation, and cut in half. Form 2 round loaves and place them on a lightly greased baking sheet or pan. Cover with a damp cloth and let rise until double in bulk, 60 minutes. Bake about 55 minutes in a 375° F. oven, thump crust, brush top with butter or your own topping, and cool on rack away from drafts.

"Take the world as it is, not as it ought to be."—German saying

Pumpernickel Bread

The history of our pumpernickel recipe begins long before our great country was in swaddling clothes. The two families of Rahn and Braué baked this healthful bread in Holland and in Schleswig-Holstein during many periods of peace and war. Even before my father sailed for the United States, he baked for the Kaiser during the black conscription days of imperialistic Germany. It is fascinating to think of how many families depended on this daily bread. It is the bread of all walks of life, truly the staff of life. Dad brought a starter batch with him when he came to America!

The secrets of texture, taste, and firmness of this bread of health are here. (You will note this recipe produces no Schwarz-brot or sour mix.) Be sure to have a large bowl, bowl knife, and greased pans. For 6 or more large loaves of healthful pumpernickel, prepare the mix, or batch, in usual white-bread manner.

1. Combine 4 cups scalded milk, ½ cup sugar, 3 tablespoons salt, 6 tablespoons lard. Stir until dissolved and lukewarm.

2. Soften 2 cakes of compressed yeast in ½ cup warm water. Add yeast, plus 3½ cups warm water, to cooled milk mixture.

3. Sift and measure 4 pounds (4 quarts) good white flour into a mixed, and remixed 2 pounds flour blend of good rye and bran flours. Blend well. Add half the flour blend to the yeast mixture; mix well; then add remaining half of the flour blend, and continue to mix well until consistency is one which "will not stick to elbow."

4. After being mixed to satisfaction, mold into balls immediately. Shape them into loaves, and place in greased pans. (Rub pans with oil-saturated cloth or paper, butter wrapper.) Let loaves rise in pans at 80°–85° F. for 2 hours, until impression of finger stays in loaves. Bake in oven of 400°–425° F. for 15 minutes; then reduce to 380° F. for the remainder of 1 hour.

Remember, friends, small loaves need less baking, while large loaves need more and hotter baking. Frankly, 'tis the feel of the mix, and the practice of making this fine bread, which will give the result its firmness and taste. Give it a good trial!

Braué's Suderstapel Rye Bread

(*Pumpernickel*)

3 packages active dry yeast (or home yeast)
2 cups warm water
4 teaspoons salt
½ cup molasses
1 to 3 tablespoons caraway seed (you may not care for this taste)
2 tablespoons soft shortening (your choice of dietary or shortening ingredient)
2 cups unsifted coarse rye meal, or
3 cups rye flour (here, again, is a great chance for a blend of flours, i.e., bran, graham, whole-wheat, rye, white and stoneground)
4 cups sifted all-purpose white flour

Dissolve yeast in water in large mixing bowl. Stir in salt, molasses, and caraway seed. Add shortening and half the flour mixture. (First mix and remix the flours in large bowl for perfect blend.) Then mix with large spoon or mixer; add rest of flour mix, and mix with hands.

Turn onto lightly floured board. Knead until satiny-smooth (can't stress this too much). Round dough up in a greased bowl, completely. Cover with a damp cloth. Place in warm place, let rise until 'tis double in bulk—nearly 2 hours. Punch dough down; cut into equal parts. Round into smooth balls, place on a floured, corn-meal-sprinkled, or poppy-seeded baking sheet or pan.

Cover with a damp cloth and let rise for 30 to 40 minutes. Brush tops of loaves lightly with cold water or butter. Bake in hot oven (450° F.) for 10 minutes, reduce heat to 350° F., and bake nearly 50 minutes longer.

The following several recipes are Dad's prize-winning breads: Starters and sponges, superior mixes for your starters and blends.

Dad's Eggless, Milkless Brown Bread

A special diet, quick-mix, pumpernickel-flavored bread that is superb with spreads and cheese—society-lady mix!

2 packages active dry yeast
3 cups warm water
1 tablespoon salt
1 tablespoon sugar
1 tablespoon shortening

3 cups all-purpose flour,
blended with
2 cups rye flour
2 cups graham flour

Dissolve yeast in water in large mixing bowl. Set aside while you mix shortening, salt, and sugar in another bowl. Add shortening mix to yeast water, then gradually add the flour blend, stirring the while, beating until smooth.

Cover with a clean cloth, and let rise in a warm place for at least 90 minutes. Turn out onto a floured board or table, knead until you feel you are the master, that it "does not stick to you." Cut in half, mold into balls, shape into loaves, and place in a greased square pan. Cover, let rise for an hour, and bake in a 400° F. oven a bit over 1 hour.

Dad's Jewish Light Rye Bread

Baked for our good Jewish friends on Broadway between Eighth and Ninth in Council Bluffs.

Sour:
1 package active dry yeast (or 2 cups starter or home yeast)
1 cup water, warm
2 cups rye flour

Dissolve yeast in water. Mix in flour. Cover, and let stand for 24 hours.

Sponge:
1 package active dry yeast (or starter)
1 cup water, warm
3 cups rye flour

Dissolve yeast in water, and mix in flour. Add to preparatory sour mixture and mix to a fine consistency. Cover, and let rise for 2 hours.

Dough:
1 tablespoon salt
1 cup water, warm
1 tablespoon malt
couple of dabs of caraway seeds, ground (optional)
2 cups unbleached flour (or all-purpose), blended with
1 cup rye flour

Mix all ingredients and add to sponge; completely incorporate but do not overmix. Scale (weigh), round up dough, and let it recover for a few moments. Make it up into long or round loaves and place on corn-mealed pans or earthenware. Proof for 12 minutes. Dock and bake in a moist 375° F. oven for 55 minutes.

Try both light and dark rye flours for variety. It is all in where one was reared; the Bavarian likes the dark rye taste.

"Life's greatest achievement is the continual remaking of yourself so that at last you know how to live."—MARK TWAIN

Dad's Old-fashioned Sour-Rye—Pumpernickel Bread

Relished by the "Five Pints"—Messrs. Damon, Johnson, Mackland, Wendt and Braué.

Mix the following together until togeddah dey schtday. ¼ cup warm water, 1 package yeast (preferably your own preparation, *nicht wahr?*), ½ cup rye flour. Cover with a plastic bag, or a clean tea towel, and let stand overnight in a warm place.

Awaken to a clean yeast smell, and mix into the overnight starter 1 cup warm water and 1 cup of rye flour. Let ferment 4 hours longer, covered. Reserve ¼ of this sour dough for another baking. (Place in a covered bowl in refrigerator, but do not freeze. When needed, add warm water and rye flour, as in foregoing step.)

Now, *achtung!* Please add to the remaining sour dough 1 package yeast (or 1 tablespoon of your own yeast preparation) dissolved in 1 cup of warm water, 2 teaspoons salt, 1 tablespoon caraway seeds (optional), 2 cups rye flour plus 2 cups of a mixture of graham, bran, white, and whole-wheat flours, or all rye meal, if pumpernickel type bread is wished.

Mix until dough is smooth and pliable. Cover with clean cloth or plastic, and place in warm place to rise for nearly an hour, or until double in bulk.

Turn out on lightly floured board or, if you're one of the fortunates, an old-fashioned butcher's table. Knead until satiny smooth (adding flour if need be). Mold into two round or long loaves and place on a greased baking sheet sprinkled with corn meal. Cover with a cloth, and let half rise, then bake in a 350° F. oven for nearly 90 minutes. (As these delicious loaves bake, you may brush tops with salted water—1 teaspoon salt to 1 cup water.) Remove to cool.

"Lives of great men all remind us
We can make our lives sublime,
And, departing, leave behind us
Footprints on the sands of time."
—LONGFELLOW

Dad's Dark-Sponge Rye-Pumpernickel

For der Kaiser, yedt.

Dissolve 2 tablespoons yeast in 2 cups warm water. Mix well with 2 cups rye flour, dark, if possible. Cover with a clean cloth; let stand for 2½ hours.

For a good drop (meaning sponge), mix 5 cups all-purpose flour (but, oh, szo much beddtah der unpbleached and a bit of graham flours), 4 cups rye meal, 2 cups warm water (variable), 2 tablespoons salt, 1 tablespoon malt, if possible. (But if not, sorghum or molasses are fair substitutes.)

Mix all this well, then add the sponge and mix all until smooth (do not overmix). Cover and let stand for 15 minutes.

Make up into round or long loaves, place on greased baking pans, sprinkled with corn meal, cover again, and let proof (rise in warm, steamy place) for 20 minutes. Dock (punch top of loaves with a sharp, clean spike or stick) each loaf 4 times, in different spots. Bake in a steamed (small pan of water under loaves) oven at 450° F. for 60 minutes. Cool and feel assured of your accomplishment!

My good father said, "One takes a Dutchman for what he means, not what he says." Szo, if I haven't mentioned ere this: a preheated oven, at a lower temperature, will aid your yeast-bread baking.

Dad's Danish Pumpernickel Rye
Velkommen—the Danske Iowa farmers loved this one!

SOUR-DOUGH STARTER. Your homemade yeast, now, ja wohl?! Dissolve ½ tablespoon active dry yeast in 2 cups warm water, then add 3 cups rye flour and mix well. Cover with a clean cloth, and let rise and fall in a warm place. (It sometimes takes 2½ to 3 hours to drop.) Save 1 cup of starter for the sponge and place the remainder in the refrigerator for future use.

SOUR-DOUGH SPONGE. Place 1 cup of starter in a large mixing bowl and add ½ cup of rye meal (pumpernickel rye) and 2½ cups lukewarm water. Mix well; place in a greased bowl; cover; and let stand in a warm place overnight. (Now you have a starter. Next time you may start with the sour-dough-sponge process.)

SOUR DOUGH. Since this winner is good weekend baking batch, on der morrow begins der following. Blend sour-dough sponge with 2 cups rye flour, 2 cups graham flour, ¼ cup salt, 12 cups rye meal, 6 cups warm water (variable), alternating the water and flours as you mix well. Meanwhile, dissolve 1 tablespoon active dry yeast in ¼ cup of warm water in a separate bowl. Mix everything together well, and place in a greased bowl, cover, let rise for nearly 2 hours.

Turn out on a lightly floured board, knead for 12 minutes. Form into round loaves and place into greased casserole dishes (or baking tins), cover again, let rise for a little over 15 minutes. Bake in a 375° F. oven for 90 minutes. Remove and cool on racks.

Braué's Old-Country Sweet-Sour Rye Bread

What memories of school, hikes, camping out, summer stock, with sour rye and cheese!

2 tablespoons dry yeast
3 cups water (110° F.)
1½ tablespoons salt
¼ cup sour milk
¼ cup brown sugar
2 tablespoons dark molasses
2 tablespoons shortening

1 cup dark rye flour
5 cups all-purpose flour in which is blended
2 cups rye meal
½ tablespoon caraway seed (optional)

Dissolve yeast in water in large bowl; add all of the ingredients except the flours, blending well; stir in rest of ingredients, mixing well for a smooth mixture. Cover with a clean cloth, let rise in a warm place for an hour.

Turn out on lightly floured board, shape into loaves, place in greased pans; cover and let rise for a few moments. Place pans in cookie pan of water and bake in steamy oven for 1 hour at 360° F.

Braué's Saxony Rye Bread

A blue-ribbon eggless, wheatless recipe for special meals of unusual taste.

Tante Carrie's Variation:

2 packages active' dry yeast	home yeast
2 cups milk, scalded	sour cream or potato soup
2 tablespoons sugar	honey or syrup
1 tablespoon salt	garlic or onion salts
2 tablespoons shortening	bacon grease
6 cups rye flour	a blend of rye, whole-wheat, unbleached flours, bran, and oatmeal

Dissolve yeast in half the milk (lukewarm) in large mixing bowl while you mix the rest of the milk, shortening, salt, and sugar in another bowl. Spoon milk-shortening mixture into milk-yeast bowl, stirring well; then add enough dry flour to make a thick batter.

Turn out onto rye-floured table or board and knead thoroughly. Shape into loaf for greased pan (or floured earthenware), brush top with shortening (if wished), cover, let rise not too high in der varhm pblaze, bake in a 375° F. oven for 1 hour. Remove to cool on rack.

Grossmutter's Old-Country Rye Bread

Another of my matriarch grandmother's Frau Fest rye variations.

2 packages active dry yeast	2 tablespoons caraway seeds (optional)
1 cup warm water	
½ cup molasses	1 tablespoon shortening
¼ cup cocoa	2 cups rye flour
1 tablespoon salt	4 cups all-purpose flour (or soya, white, unbleached flours)
2 cups water, lukewarm (variable)	

Dissolve yeast in warm water in a large mixing bowl. Set aside while you blend the flours thoroughly, also mit der cocoa yedt, in another bowl. Combine molasses, salt, caraway seeds, and lukewarm water, stir well, in yet another bowl. Then back to yeast-water mixture bowl. Spoon in molasses mixture, cut in shortening, and add flour, stirring to a soft dough.

Turn out onto a lightly floured board; knead until dough becomes elastically smooth. Spoon, or "bowl-knife," dough into greased bowl, turn over once, cover, and let rise until doubled in bulk.

Punch down, turn out to lightly floured board, shape into ball, cut in half, mold into loaves (round or long).

Place in greased pans, if long; on greased sheet, if round. Cover; let rise for an hour; bake in 375° F. oven for 50 minutes; turn out on racks to cool.

Dad's Schleswig Rye-Wheat Buttermilk Bread

I have a feeling this bread brought the Rahns and Braués together, family-wise, for we enjoyed its mouth-watering goodness on many occasions. Our Dakota farmer relations baked it for us often.

2 packages active dry yeast (or 2 cakes compressed yeast)
2 teaspoons salt
½ cup warm water (110° F.)
2 cups buttermilk, lukewarm
1 cup light molasses (sorghum, if you wish)
2 tablespoons caraway seeds (the youngsters may object, but try it)
¼ cup melted shortening (corn oil)
3 cups sifted all-purpose flour
3 cups each unsifted rye and whole-wheat flour (a good chance to experiment—try soy flour)

Dissolve yeast in water and let stand until buttermilk heats to lukewarm. Pour buttermilk into large bowl along with yeast mixture, molasses, caraway seeds, salt, and shortening. Then add white, rye, and whole-wheat flours, stirring or beating all the while until satiny smooth. Turn twice in greased bowl, cover with clean cloth, let rise in a warm place for the doubling-in-size process. Cut, shape in loaves, place in greased bread pans, let rise until doubled, then bake in 325° F. oven until "thumping done"—50 minutes.

Dad's Old-Country Buttermilk Rye Bread

This unique loaf combines subtle flavor with nutrition in its compactness.

1 package active dry yeast
2 cups buttermilk (heat to warm—normal milk separation may result)
1 cup molasses
¼ cup shortening, melted
1 tablespoon caraway seeds (optional; or more, if desired)
2 teaspoons salt
2 cups all-purpose flour
2 cups rye flour
2 cups whole-wheat flour (blend salt and all flours well)

Dissolve yeast in warm buttermilk in large mixing bowl. Stir in molasses, shortening, and caraway seeds. Gradually add flour and salt mixture, beating well to correct kneading consistency. Turn out onto floured table or board and knead until "elastically smooth and alive." Place in greased bowl, turn over once, cover, let rise until doubled in bulk (over 1 hour).

Punch dough down, turn out onto floured board, cut in half, mold into rounds or longs, place on greased sheets (or earthenware tiles), and cover with damp cloth. Let rise for an hour, then diagonally slash tops of loaves. Bake in 350° F. oven for 1 hour.

Father's Unleavened Dark Bread

A delightful hand-me-down—drop buns, too!

2 cups stock (or milk or water)
1 cup oil (nutritional or vegetable oil)
1 teaspoon salt
8 cups whole-wheat flour (or a blend of rye and dark flours and unbleached white or all-purpose flour)

Beat the oil and stock or liquid until it has the appearance of a playful tide on the beach. Gradually add the flour over the liquid, together with the salt. Beat well. Turn out on a lightly floured board and knead until elastically smooth. Cover and let stand overnight in a warm place.

In the good morning knead lightly again. Divide into 2 equal portions and place each in a greased bread pan.

Bake at 350° F. for at least 90 minutes. Take out and cool on rack.

Bernadotte's Swedish Limpa (Rye) Bread

Named after the great Swedish dynasty. The Swedes are not only constant neutralists, but thorough traders. This trade was consummated with one of Father's Swedish buddies when they baked Schwarzbrot for the Kaiser in the Imperial Army.

2 packages active dry yeast
2 cups warm water
¼ cup molasses
⅓ cup sugar
1 tablespoon salt
2 tablespoons orange rind, grated
1 tablespoon fennel seeds, crushed (pestle and mortar)
2 tablespoons anise seeds, crushed (mortar-fine, as fennel seeds)
2 tablespoons shortening
3 cups all-purpose flour, blended with
3 cups rye flour

Dissolve yeast in warm water in large mixing bowl while you blend all the dry ingredients and orange rind in another bowl. Add molasses and shortening to the yeast water, then gradually add the flour blend, constantly stirring. Beat until satiny smooth.

Turn out onto floured board and knead for 6 minutes, until elastic. Then place in greased bowl, turn dough over once, cover with a damp cloth, and let rise in a warm place until doubled in bulk.

Punch dough down, turn out on lightly floured board, cut in half, and shape into tapered or oval loaves. Place on greased sheets (or earthenware), cover with a damp cloth, let rise for an hour. Diagonally gash tops of loaves and bake in a 375° F. oven for nearly 40 minutes. Cool on rack.

My Father's Original German Sour Bread

A family favorite—once baked for high- and low-born alike.

1 cup sour-dough starter
2 quarts potato water (lukewarm to room temperature)
2 tablespoons salt
½ cup molasses (or honey, syrup, sorghum)
¼ cup nutritional yeast (brewers' yeast), optional
2 tablespoons caraway seeds, whole
1 cup dry milk (or milk of your choice; cut down a bit on your
    potato water if liquid milk)
10 cups rye flour (variable)

Mix sour-dough starter with the liquids and half the rye
flour. Cover and let stand in a warm spot at least 3 hours. (The
longer it stands the more sour it becomes.)

Stir; reserve and refrigerate 1 cup of this starter for your
next baking. Combine the rest of the mixture with all the other
ingredients to make a dough of good consistency, though stiff.
Turn out on a lightly floured board and knead until no longer
sticky. Divide and mold into equal loaves, round or long, and
place on a greased baking sheet (or earthenware). Cover with
a damp cloth and place in a humid, warm place to rise for 4
hours.

Bake in a 350° F. oven (dry or humid) for 90 minutes. Sour
dough is a slow riser.

Grossmutter's All-Rye Bread

**Grandmother's Kaffee Klatsch Bread (with the ladies), plus the
daily, old-country "Schpech" and "Smierkase."**

2 packages active dry yeast
    (or 2 cups starter)
1 cup warm water (variable)
2 cups milk, scalded
1 tablespoon salt
3 tablespoons brown sugar
3 tablespoons shortening

2 tablespoons caraway seeds
    (optional, soaked in cold
    water)
1 cup cold water (der cara-
    way seed soaken)
6 cups rye flour

Dissolve yeast in warm water in large mixing bowl. Let stand while you combine milk, sugar, salt, and shortening in another bowl. Stir well and add caraway and water. Stir to lukewarm, and add to yeast mixture, stirring the while. Add half the flour, beating well; then pour in rest of flour until dough is stiff but workable.

Turn out on lightly floured board (rye-floured), and knead for nearly 12 minutes, or until dough "yumps back like a glacier" (wisely stated by one of Dad's helpers) at knuckle touch.

Place in greased bowl, turn over once, cover with tea towel, let rise in a warm place for nearly an hour. Punch down with fist(s), cut and shape into loaves. Place in greased bread pans, cover, let rise again for an hour, and bake in a 400° F. oven for 15 minutes. Lower heat to 375° F. and bake until golden brown, for 40 minutes.

"Governments, like clocks, go from the motion men give them, and governments are made and moved by men, so by them they are ruled also. Therefore, governments depend upon men rather than men upon governments."—WILLIAM PENN

Missouri Valley Light Swedish Limpa

Limpa sweet bread, the favorite of the north-south train runs.

2 tablespoons yeast (and a bit of starter, if you wish)
2 cups of warm water, variable
1 tablespoon brown sugar (packed)
2 tablespoons shortening (butter, margarine or oil)
1 teaspoon caraway seeds (ground, optional)
1 teaspoon grated orange peel
4 cups all-purpose flour (or unbleached or white), variable
2 cups of rye flour
2 cups white flour *not* blended with other flour
2 teaspoons salt

Dissolve yeast in the water in large mixing bowl. Set aside while, in another bowl, you mix the rest of the ingredients (the flour should be first blended together) except for salt and 2 cups white flour, blending well. Pour the yeast water into the flour mixture, adding slowly, stirring the while. Mix to a soft sponge.

Cover with a clean cloth, place in warm place, and let rise and drop (nearly an hour).

When the sponge is ready, add 2 cups of white flour and 2 teaspoons of salt to sponge and mix until satiny smooth. Cover, let rise for another hour. Turn out onto a lightly floured board, round up into loaves, cover. Let loaves rest for 15 minutes. Place on greased sheets (earthenware) and bake in 425° F. oven for 45 minutes.

"Liberty lies in the hearts of men and women; when it dies there, no constitution, no law, no court can save it."

—JUDGE LEARNED HAND

CASSEROLE BREADS

Before Father's passing away, in his beloved bakery in 1940, the "enriched flour" and no-knead breads had become quite popular, and Father was often called upon to bake these herb casserole breads. ("Pot brots" was Dad's name for them.) He baked these moisty peasant pleasantries in cast-iron, or crock, pots and bowls. Here are a few of the Braué Home Bakery sensations. (I shall present them all as electric-mixer recipes, but if you still are of the hand-wooden-spoon mixing method, please do so—one hundred vigorous strokes a minute.)

"Patience is the companion of wisdom."—SAINT AUGUSTINE

Braué's Swedish Limpa (Rye) Pot Brot

There are many variations on this barely sweet rye bread of justifiable festive fame, but the following is what my father and his good Swedish friend loved to bake year after year. Many a loaf went down with the Swedish Line.

3 tablespoons dry yeast (or 4 cups starter)
¼ cup warm water
¼ cup molasses
1 tablespoon caraway seeds (optional)
2 tablespoons shortening (or butter, margarine)
2 tablespoons grated orange peel (or 1 tablespoon anise seed)
1 teaspoon each of crushed fennel seeds and cumin seeds (optional)
½ cup cracked wheat
3 cups water
1 cup warm milk
6 cups whole-wheat flour (or whole-wheat–white mix)
2 teaspoons salt
4 cups rye flour

Dissolve yeast in warm water. Set aside while you mix together and boil for about 2 minutes 3 cups water, cracked wheat, seeds, orange peel, molasses, and shortening. Cool to lukewarm, add milk, and stir in whole-wheat flour.

Mix to make a soft dough, cover, and let rise for a little over 1 hour.

Mix in rye flour and salt to make a stiff dough, cover, and let rise for 2 hours. Knead slightly, shape into loaves for greased bread pans or casseroles, cover, and let rise for 20 minutes.

Bake in 350° F. oven for 50 minutes. Remove from pans and cool on racks.

One variation in mixing steps could be: Instead of a soft dough, blend all flours and salt, mix to make a stiff dough, cover, and let rise until doubled in bulk, knead and shape into loaves.

Braué's Home Banana Rye Pot Brot

Before World War II, my father was in the health-food business, but good. His flavorful, healthful breads were recommended by leading physicians. This tender, delicious loaf is for people allergic to eggs, wheat, and milk.

2 packages active dry yeast
1 cup warm water
1 tablespoon salt
2 tablespoons sugar (a little less)
3 tablespoons shortening (oil, margarine, butter, lard), melted
3 cups ripe bananas (brown-flecked yellow peel), mashed (or 6 good bananas)
6 cups rye flour (if you are not allergic, try your hand at blending flours)

Dissolve yeast in warm water in large mixing bowl while in another bowl you mix together half the flour and all the rest of the ingredients. Spoon into yeast water and mix well, gradually adding, stirring, the rest of flour. Mix until smooth, adding flour and water if needed. Turn out onto a rye-floured board, knead for nearly 10 minutes (be sure it is not sticky), place in greased bowl, turn over once, cover, let rise in warm place for nearly 2 hours.

Turn out on floured board again and knead lightly for 3 minutes. Mold into round loaves and place in greased casseroles or pots (cast iron is perfect), cover with damp cloth, let rise for an hour.

Bake in 425° F. oven for 12 minutes, lower temperature to 350° F. and bake for 45 more minutes. Remove bread to racks, brush tops with water (optional). Serve with gusto!

"What's past help is beyond prevention."—Massinger

Braué's Pastors' Delight Anise Braunbrot

The members of the Ministerial Alliance loved it.

2 packages dry yeast
2 cups warm water
2 cups whole-wheat flour or graham-bran mixture
3 cups all-purpose flour
2 tablespoons honey, and
a touch of your favorite syrup (both optional)

3 tablespoons soft butter, or margarine
2 teaspoons ("plus a dash") of salt
2 teaspoons crushed anise seed

Dissolve yeast in water in electric-mixer bowl. In another mixing bowl, combine and thoroughly mix flours. Add salt, honey, butter, and half the flour to the yeast mixture. Blend, at mixer's low speed; then beat at medium speed until satiny-smooth, for about "drei minuten yedt." Add rest of flour and blend thoroughly at medium speed for two impatient minutes. Scrape sides of bowl and beaters with rubber scraper, then give it a few turns with a wooden spoon. Cover bowl with plastic or waxed paper and clean cloth and let rise in a draftless warm place for nearly an hour.

Meanwhile, back at the oven, you have preheated the blighter to 350° F. Lightly sprinkle your greased 2-quart casserole on inside bottom and sides with 1 teaspoon anise seed. Stir batter while you recite the alphabet and sprinkle the batter with the rest of anise seed.

Bake for a little less than 1 hour, remove to rack, and serve in warm wedges!

Herr Braué's German Farmers' Herb-Parmesan-Egg Bread

Buffet par excellence, sliced thin or toasted.

2 packages active dry yeast
2 cups warm water
1 tablespoon sugar
2 teaspoons salt
5 cups all-purpose flour (another chance to blend flours, un-bleached, whole-wheat, rye, etc.)
1 egg white, beaten yust slightly yedt
1 tablespoon water at room temperature
a few sesame seeds; optional
1 teaspoon oregano mixed with
½ teaspoon seasoning salt or garlic salt
½ cup chopped parsley (or a touch of bay leaves)
½ cup grated Parmesan cheese (or your favorite cheese); let stand for quite a spell

Dissolve yeast in warm water while you mix herb-cheese combination. Stir sugar, salt and half the flour into the yeast mixture. Beat vigorously while you stir in remaining flour (medium speed for nearly 2 minutes, or 200 strokes with your spoon). Turn out onto lightly floured board and knead until elastically smooth. Turn into greased bowl, turn over once, cover with a clean cloth, and let rise in warm place for a bit over 30 minutes.

Punch dough down, turn it out onto lightly floured board, and roll it out into rectangle. Sprinkle with the herb-cheese mixture, roll up from narrow end into a roll, pinch seams and place seam down into a large greased bread pan.

Cover with a clean cloth, and let rise until doubled in bulk. You may wish smaller loaves; if so, cut dough in half, roll out into rectangle, cut into thirds. Repeat with second half, then do as with large loaf (above), place all in large bread, or cake, pan.

Bake in 375° F. oven for 30 minutes. Remove from oven and brush with egg-white–water mixture and, if desired, sprinkle with a few sesame seeds. Back to der bake oven for another 30 minutes. Remove and cool on racks. Makes 1 large loaf, or 6 small loaves, or 2 or 3 loaves.

"Travel teaches toleration."—DISRAELI

Uncle Hans's Schleswig-Holstein Farmers' Onion-Dill-Cheese Loaf

No kneading or shaping . . . ideal for the busy mother-daughter duo . . . a gem for the young folks' buffets (young at heart, too, of course). Slice, or break, warm from the rack, and you will agree these are the most subtle and intriguing loaves to supplement cole slaw, seafoods, cold cuts, und so weiter.

1 cake compressed yeast (or 1 package active dry yeast, or 3 cups starter)
1 cup warm water
2 tablespoons sugar (or honey)
1 cup farmers' creamy cottage cheese (smierkase), heated to lukewarm
1 tablespoon minced onion (packaged, instant, or your preparation)
2 teaspoons dill seed (or weed)
1 teaspoon salt
1 egg
¼ teaspoon baking soda
5 cups all-purpose flour (but, oh, so much der beddah mit unbleached flour with a touch of rye flour)
½ cup butter, margarine, or corn oil

Dissolve yeast in the water in a large bowl and set aside while you mix all other ingredients, except cheese, in another large bowl. Stir cheese into yeast mixture. Spoon flour mixture into cheese-yeast mixture, and beat or mix vigorously until dough is sticky-heavy. Cover with a clean cloth and in der varhm geputten for nearly an hour.

Punch and stir dough down. Spoon into casserole deep dish, cover again, and let rise till 'tis doubled.

Bake in a 350° F. oven for nearly 1 hour. Brush top with butter, remove from dish; cut or break in half or in quarters.

"What one has, one ought to use."—CICERO

Council Bluffs' Favorite Back-Yard Herb Pot Brot

Okay patio, this day and age! Another of Dad's prize casserole breads.

2 packages active dry yeast
2 cups warm water
2 teaspoons salt
2 tablespoons sugar
2 tablespoons soft or melted butter or margarine (or your favorite oil, or Iowa corn oil)
1 tablespoon dried rosemary leaves (or your favorite herb—one may experiment with herbs too, and become an expert, as with flours
6 cups all-purpose flour (unbleached-soya-white flour mixture)

Dissolve yeast in warm water in large bowl. Let stand while you blend all the dry ingredients in another bowl. Stir in butter first, then flour mixture into yeast bowl and beat at medium speed (when in doubt with electric mixer, the casserole doughs take about 2 minutes) until completely blended and satiny smooth. Scrape down sides of bowl, cover with a clean cloth, and let rise until doubled in bulk and bubbly.

Stir down dough fast for a dozen strokes, then turn into greased 2-quart casserole (pot or ware), and bake in 375° F. oven for nearly an hour. Cool on rack, or serve warmish.

Sister Phoebe's Raisin Batter Pot Brot

One of Mother's first recipes—baked for her older sisters as a "growing-up test."

1 package active dry yeast (or homemade yeast food)
1 cup warm water
1 cup milk, scalded
¼ cup shortening
1 tablespoon sugar
1 teaspoon salt (a bit over a teaspoon)

1 egg, mixed with
1 teaspoon cinnamon
2 teaspoons orange rind, grated
1 cup raisins, seedless
5 cups all-purpose flour (variable—Mother would blend dark flours with white flour)

Dissolve yeast in warm water in large mixing bowl. Set aside while you combine milk, shortening, sugar, and salt in another bowl. Mix well, cool to lukewarm. Add the egg mixture to the milk mixture, stirring the while, then to the yeast-water bowl, and beat well (200 to 300 hand strokes, or 2 to 3 minutes at medium speed). Gradually stir in flour and raisins, beating until dough is creamy smooth.

Spoon batter into 2-quart casserole (or earthenware or cast-iron pot), cover with a clean damp cloth, and let rise in warm place for an hour. Bake in a 350° F. oven for at least 45 minutes (depends on oven). Remove from pot, cool on rack, and decorate with your favorite or confectioners' frosting.

CONFECTIONERS' FROSTING. Blend well 1 cup confectioners' sugar, 2 tablespoons milk, cream, or water, and 1 teaspoon almond (or vanilla) extract. Plenty caloric!

Dad's Modern Casserole Bread

A forerunner of the present popular patio loaves . . . baked for the society lady of "time is of the essence" fame.

2 packages active dry yeast
1 cup warm water
3 tablespoons sugar
1 tablespoon salt
1 cup lukewarm milk
2 tablespoons shortening (butter, margarine, or oil)
7 cups all-purpose flour (or a mixture of soya, bran, unbleached flours blended with an herb flavoring of chopped parsley, chives, and thyme, ¼ teaspoon each)

Dissolve yeast in water and let soak for a few minutes while, in another bowl, you pour the milk over salt, sugar, and shortening. Stir until dissolved. Pour milk mixture into yeast mixture, stir while you add flour. Beat well with a wooden spoon or mixer.

Cover bowl with greased wax paper or a clean cloth; let rise for 45 minutes. Punch down with spoon; beat vigorously two dozen times. Spoon into a greased 2-quart casserole (or cast-iron or earthenware pot). Bake in 375° F. oven for an hour.

Tante Wilhelmina's Rye Pot Brot

This batch has won prizes since the early Saxon Duchy Fair days. Easy to mix, easy to bake, truly a favorite with youth, in-laws, and out-laws (out of family).

2 packages active dry yeast
1 cup warm water
1 cup milk, scalded
2½ teaspoons salt
¼ cup brown sugar, dark and firmly packed
2 tablespoons butter, margarine, or oil (or shortening)
4 cups all-purpose flour (unbleached, soya, and white flours)
2 cups rye flour (blend with above flours)
a bit of egg white and water, or milk, for topping

Dissolve yeast in water in mixing bowl. Set aside while you blend and stir milk, salt, sugar, and butter in another bowl. Let cool to lukewarm; then stir into yeast mixture as you gradually also stir in the flour mixture. Beat for nearly 3 minutes, until fully blended.

Cover with a clean cloth, let rise in a warm place until doubled in bulk (nearly an hour). Stir down with a wooden spoon and beat for 30 seconds. Spoon into lightly greased 2-quart casserole.

Brush with topping and bake in a 375° F. oven for an hour, or until thumpingly done. Remove to rack to cool.

Braué's Italian Peasant Bread

A casserole loaf loved by the G.I.'s of both sides—presented to a Rahn long ago during a lull in the mountain campaigns.

2 packages active dry yeast
2 cups warm water
2 teaspoons salt
2 tablespoons sugar
2 tablespoons butter, margarine, melted (or oil of your choice)
1 package Italian spaghetti sauce mix (other mixes work well; the original sauce will be included in another book)
6 cups all-purpose flour (or unbleached, rye, and white flours)

Dissolve yeast in warm water, stir, and let stand. In another bowl blend salt, sugar, butter, sauce mix, and half the flour. Add this mixture to the yeast water, and beat until satiny smooth (slowly, then faster with mixer—vigorously with spoon.) Scrape down sides of bowl; then with wooden spoon beat in rest of flour until fully blended.

Cover with clean cloth and let rise in warm place until doubled in bubbly bulk.

Lightly grease a 2-quart casserole or pot. Spoon down batter, vigorously beat for two dozen strokes, turn into casserole, and bake in 375° F. oven for nearly an hour. Remove to rack to cool, or serve warm in wedge style.

"When one will not, two cannot quarrel."—Spanish saying

Braué's Suderstapel German Bread

A caloric delicacy handed down from daughter to daughter—a courtin' loaf.

2 packages dry yeast, or homemade yeast
1 cup warm water
1 cup scalded milk
½ cup butter, other shortening
1 cup honey
1 teaspoon salt
2 well-beaten eggs
6 cups all-purpose flour (un-bleached; if wished, your chance to experiment)

Topping Ingredients:
1½ cups soft bread crumbs
3 tablespoons light brown sugar
¼ teaspoon salt
1 teaspoon cinnamon
2 tablespoons melted butter

Dissolve yeast in warm water, set aside while in another bowl you stir together butter, salt, honey, and milk. (Be sure butter is melted.) Stir 1 cup of flour into milk mixture, then the yeast mixture. Mix in the eggs and remaining flour (hand or wooden-spoon mix). Beat well.

Cover with a clean cloth, let rise in der varhm pblace yedt for nearly 90 minutes, beat well again. Mix topping mixture together while mix-batter is rising. Grease and lightly flour a square cake pan or a casserole bowl. Turn batter into pan or bowl und shpringkle der top den mitt der topping migxture yedt.

Cover again, let rise until doubled in bulk. Bake in a 350° F. oven for nearly 30 minutes. Girls, a perfect loaf for that man!

"The government is similar to a loving wife: we may (do) disagree with her quite frequently, but we have no intention of leaving her." —A government employee—a voter

Dad's Back-Yard Onion Pot Brot

This evokes memories of heavily laden tables of home-cooked, home-baked foods mit der relazhuns back of der haus grouped.

2 packages dry yeast
2 cups warm water
2 tablespoons sugar
2 teaspoons salt
2 tablespoons melted butter, margarine, or salad oil
1 diced onion (your favorite), or a package of onion soup or salad mix, dry, or French onion soup stock
6 cups all-purpose flour (or unbleached flour mixed with a touch of white and rye flours)

Dissolve yeast in water and let stand, while you mix all the other ingredients thoroughly in another bowl. Spoon flour mixture into yeast mixture and beat at low speed for a couple of minutes, then to medium speed until dough is smooth.

Cover bowl with clean cloth, and let rise in warm place until doubled in bulk (50 minutes). Preheat oven to 350° F. and grease a 2-quart casserole lightly. Beat batter for 30 seconds, a stroke a second, then spoon into casserole.

Bake for 1 hour, or until "bread-brown." Remove to rack to cool; serve in warm wedges.

"All authority belongs to the people."—JEFFERSON

Braué's German-Lutheran Special
Dill-Olive Pot Brot

A hospitable touch with the informal pleasantness of the patio.

2 packages active dry yeast
2 cups warm water
2 teaspoons salt
2 tablespoons sugar (or honey)
2 tablespoons shortening, butter, or margarine, softened (or oil)
2 tablespoons dill weed, dried
3 tablespoons stuffed olives (Spanish), chopped and drained
6 cups all-purpose flour (or unbleached, whole-wheat, and white flours)
a touch bit of dill seed

Dissolve yeast in mixer bowl with water. Let stand while you blend salt, sugar, butter, dill weed, olives, and half the flour in another bowl. Spoon this mixture into yeast water and beat, first at low, then at medium speed for 3 minutes (hand or spoon beating if you prefer, naturlich), until satiny smooth. Scrape down bowl with bowl scraper. Beat in rest of flour with wooden spoon until fully blended.

Cover with a clean tea towel, let rise in warm place until doubled in bulk and bubbly (nearly an hour). Lightly grease your 2-quart casserole (pot or earthenware), spoon down batter, stir vigorously for two dozen strokes, and turn into casserole. Lightly sprinkle batter with dill seed.

Bake for one hour in 375° F. oven. Remove from casserole, cool on rack, or serve in warm wedges to the impatients.

"Life is always flowing on like a river, sometimes with murmurs, sometimes without bending this way and that, we do not exactly see why, now in beautiful picturesque places, now through barren and uninteresting scenes, but always flowing with a look of treachery about it; it is so swift, so voiceless, yet so continuous."—FABER

Old-Country Schpeck Pot Brot

A memorable loaf for patio dinners. Let the younger set experiment on these breads, from beginning to end a great chance for expression!

2 packages active dry yeast
2 cups warm water (110° F.)
6 cups all-purpose flour (or unbleached, preferably)
2 tablespoons sugar
2 teaspoons salt
¼ cup chopped green pepper (or chopped Spanish olives)
2 tablespoons chopped pimiento (or 1 tablespoon pimiento cheese)
1 dozen slices lean bacon (sauté bacon before you mix any of the ingredients, drain bacon well)
bacon drippings
1 cup boiling water
1 cup yellow corn meal

Dissolve yeast in warm water while bacon is cooking on medium heat. In your large electric mixer bowl, pour the boiling water over salt, drippings, sugar, and ½ cup corn meal, and stir slowly but well. Add yeast mixture, always stirring. Add half the flour, beat at low speed for blending, then at medium speed until satiny-smooth. Stir in crumbled bacon and rest of ingredients and flour until fully blended.

Turn over batch and cover. Let rise in a warm place until dough is "bubbly doubled." Lightly grease a 2-quart casserole (or your favorite ole pot) and sprinkle sides and bottom with corn meal. Stir down batch and beat it 30 times with meaning.

Spoon into casserole, sprinkle with corn meal, and bake in a 350° F. oven for 1 hour, or until brown it is. Cool on rack, or serve warm.

"A bank is a place where they lend you an umbrella in fair weather and ask for it back again when it begins to rain."
—ROBERT FROST

Daddy's Rebel-Yankee Hominy Bread

This tasty surprise brought brothers and "others" together once more. (Brought back from "the War" by a General Lee Hawkeye!)

2 cups hominy grits, cooked, warm (variable)
¼ teaspoon salt
1½ tablespoon shortening, melted (or nutritional oil, etc.)
2 cups milk
2 egg yolks, beaten
2 egg whites, beaten

Mix well the hominy grits, salt, and shortening. Add and incorporate thoroughly (bakers' talk) milk and egg yolks, mixing well. Fold in egg whites, stirring well.

Spoon into greased casserole (or earthenware) dish and bake in 400° F. oven for 40 to 45 minutes. Serve in casserole.

"The thinking is man's—the knowing is God's."

CORN BREADS

Corn meal, the gift of the American Indian to the early Pilgrim settlers, has stirred up a great deal of controversy between the North and the South. Although not the cause of the "war between the states," it has had its repercussions. Southerners believe that sugar should not be mixed in corn bread and prefer white corn meal, while the northerners feel that yellow corn meal is better and sugar will make it a very crusty type of corn bread. (Oh, will I ever hear about this!) Many tall Texans feel that creamed corn must be mixed in the batter for the "blessing good taste!"

Lack of space has decreed that Uncle John must depart from the history of corn meal (mayhap more in a later edition), sooo, in spite of past events, corn meal results in a tantalizing loaf when combined with other grain flours, or "as you like it." One cup of flour is the baker's equivalent of a bit less than a cup of corn meal.

Braué's Hawkeye-Cornhuskers' Spoon Bread

Many loaves were "broken" during Iowa-Nebraska games. Superior with milk, cocoa and coffee. (Wrap in tea towel.)

1 package active dry yeast (starter)
1 cup water, warm
1 cup milk, scalded
1 tablespoon oil (nutritional or your choice)
2 tablespoons honey (or raw sugar, a bit more)
1 teaspoon salt
1 egg, beaten
4 cups whole-wheat flour (variable) and corn meal, mixed

Dissolve the yeast in warm water in a large mixing bowl. Add milk, oil, egg, honey, and salt. Stir well and add the flour mixture gradually and incorporate well. Cover and let rise for 30 minutes.

Stir down and spoon into greased pans. Cover again and let rise for 30 minutes. Bake in a 350° F. oven for 60 minutes.

"The best test of a nation's culture remains what it has always been since the days of Gutenberg: Its attitude towards books."

—ALLEN NEVINS

Braué's New England Corn-Meal Shortenin' Bread

Our good friends the railroad men used to deliver Dad's bread all over the country, and this is one of the "Neighbor, let's trade recipes" results. Several tangy morsels!

1 package active yeast (or starter)
1 cup warm water (110° F.)
2 cups water (boiling)
1 cup yellow corn meal (rolled oats for oatmeal bread)

½ cup molasses
2 teaspoons salt
6 cups sifted flour (all-purpose, but try a little soy flour)
2 tablespoons shortening

Pour boiling water into large bowl mit der corn meal slowly, then add salt, shortening, and molasses. Cool to lukewarm. (Note change in procedure; according to a Down-Easter, this is the secret.) Then place yeast in warm water and stir until completely dissolved. Add yeast water and enough flour to corn-meal mixture to make dough stiff. Turn onto lightly floured board, knead normally until dough is elastically smooth.

Place in greased bowl, cover with clean cloth; let rise in a warm place, draftless, until dough has doubled in size, about 1 hour. Cut dough in half and shape into loaves. Place in greased loaf pans, let rise again in a warm place for another hour. Bake in a hot oven (400° F.) for nearly 1 hour. Brush tops of bread with melted butter and serve proudly!

Goes great with soups and stews!

TRIED AND TRUE ADVICE. No other food presents the triple goodness of economy, nutrition, and appetite appeal. Carbohydrates for heat and energy, proteins for stamina and pep, plus the appeal of going so well with other nutritional foods—bread!

Earlene's All-American Spoon Bread

Soakingly delicious when crumbled into a tall glass of milk and eaten with a spoon (sweet milk, you all). Through this performance, I met Earlene at the Van Horn Boarding House in Odessa, Texas.

2 cups corn meal, white	1 teaspoon sugar
2 cups milk, scalded	1 teaspoon salt
2 teaspoons butter, melted	2 eggs, separated

Add the corn meal gradually to the milk, stirring constantly to prevent lumping. Cook over moderate heat for at least 15 minutes, until the mixture thickens. Add butter, sugar, and salt. Set aside for a few moments while you beat the egg yolks; spoon and stir the yolks into the corn-meal mixture. Set aside while you beat the egg whites, stiff yedt; fold them into corn-meal mixture, stirring well but slowly. Pour into a greased casserole (or cast-iron skillet), and bake in 350° F. oven for 45 minutes. Serve hot from the baking container with milk, apple butter, ham, and beans!

"Trust not him who has broken faith."—SHAKESPEARE

Dad's German Farmers' Honey-Wheat-Corn Bread

A symphony of taste blends.

2 packages active dry yeast (or starter)	1 cup corn meal blended with 1 cup whole-wheat flour and
1 cup milk, warm	1 cup soy flour
2 eggs, beaten	1 teaspoon salt
3 tablespoons honey	¼ cup nutritional yeast
3 tablespoons oil (your choice of health oils or butter)	(brewers' yeast or wheat germ)

Dissolve yeast in milk and set aside for a few moments. Blend all the other ingredients in another bowl; then mix them with the yeast-milk mixture. Spoon into a greased or oiled casserole. Set in a warm place and let rise for at least ½ hour.

Bake at 325° F. for 40 minutes. Serve from casserole in wedges.

Mother's Healthful Spoon Bread

An engaging recipe for company.

3 packages active dry yeast (starter)
1 quart milk, warm
3 tablepoons honey
1 teaspoon salt
1 cup brewers' yeast (optional, this is nutritional yeast)
10 cups of a blend of flours (whole-wheat, graham, bran, unbleached, white; and corn meal. This is a wonderful chance for experimentation)

Dissolve yeast in warm milk. Add honey. Let set until bubbly, then stir in the remaining ingredients. Stir well with a large wooden spoon. The dough will be thin, but do not despair. Spoon the mixture into a large casserole or several smaller dishes, filling one-half full.

Cover and let rise in a warm place until the dough has almost reached top of casserole. Bake in a 375° F. oven for at least 45 minutes.

Mother's Rye-Corn Bread

One of Mother's favorites.

starter dissolved in
2 cups milk, scalded (or stock or potato water)
4 cups corn meal
½ cup molasses (or honey)

2 teaspoons salt
½ cup nutritional yeast (brewers' yeast)
4 cups rye flour

Pour the milk-starter mix over the corn meal, stirring the while. Incorporate all the other ingredients, stirring slowly but well. Cover and let rise overnight.

Next morning stir the batter down. Turn out on your bread board and let it rest for a few seconds. Divide in half. Turn into greased bread pans. Smooth tops of dough with wet fingers, cover, let rest for a spell (5 to 10 minutes).

Bake in 350° F. oven for at least 35 to 40 minutes.

Juan's Tortillas

A most popular contribution to modern living by a good friend and outstanding mess sergeant. "Leedle wans" are "tostaditas," and "beeg wans" fried are "tostadas," Skipper!

2 cups corn meal, blended with
2 cups flour (unbleached), and
2 teaspoons salt

2 tablespoons lard or shortening
1 cup water, warm

Cut shortening into flour blend. Add water and stir into ball. Turn out onto lightly floured board and knead for "a spell," until smooth. Shape into baseball-size balls, and let them rest while you check your griddle or pan. Roll balls out thinner than pie dough, and cook on ungreased hot griddle, browning both sides for bread, one side only if they are to be filled and rolled.

When used as dippers, cut dough to size, sprinkle with salts, herbs, or powders, fry in shortening until crisp. Cook up ahead and reserve.

THIS YEAR'S RECIPE: *Take 12 fine full-grown months; see that these are thoroughly free from all old memories of bitterness, rancor, hate, and jealousy. Cleanse them completely from every clinging spite; pick off all specks of pettiness. Cut each month into 30 or 31 equal parts. Do not attempt to make up the whole batch at one time.*

Prepare one day at a time as follows: Into each day put equal parts of faith, patience, courage, work, hope, fidelity, liberality, kindness, rest, prayer, meditation; add about 1 teaspoonful of good spirits, a dash of fun, a pinch of folly, a sprinkling of play, and a heaping cupful of good humor. Pour love into the whole and mix with a vim.

Serve with quietness, unselfishness, and cheerfulness.

RAISIN BREADS

Raisins, dried grapes cured in the sun, made their first appearance in Europe with the Crusaders, who brought the healthful, richly sweet dried fruit home with them from the oft ill-fated Crusades. History has proved raisins more than a delicacy. They are now used in everyday dishes of nutritional value. Muscat, Sultana and Thompson grapes (grown without seeds) supply the marketed raisins.

"The groundwork of all happiness is health."—HUNT

Dad's Spicy Raisin Batter Bread

Easily created and heartily enjoyed! Many of these "winning Wednesdays" coincided with the city's church socials and greatly helped to supplement the menus.

1 package active dry yeast
2 cups warm water
2 teaspoons salt
2 tablespoons sugar
2 tablespoons soft shortening

5 cups sifted all-purpose flour
¼ teaspoon nutmeg
¼ teaspoon mace
⅛ teaspoon cloves
½ cup seedless raisins

(if you like nuts, decrease amount of raisins a bit, and add ¼ cup walnuts or your favorite nuts)

Dissolve yeast in warm water in large bowl, and add salt, sugar, shortening, and half the flour. Beat for about 3 minutes, then add the remaining flour, spices, raisins, and nuts, stirring constantly. Mix until smooth.

Cover with a clean cloth, let rise in warm place until double in size. Stir down with hand or spoon; spoon into greased loaf pan; pat with lightly floured hand. Cover with a cloth, let rise until batter is thumb joint from top of pan.

Bake in 350° F. oven for 45 minutes. Top it if you wish, but 'tis flavorful plain!

Dad's Wednesday Very-Special Citrus-Raisin Bread

A batter casserole mix that will delight the younger set at snack time or "after the game." Or let them mix and bake it for the County Fair.

2 packages active dry yeast
2 cups warm water
1 teaspoon salt
¼ cup granulated sugar
¼ cup soft butter or margarine (oil)
1 egg and the white of an egg (save the yolk for topping)
2 tablespoons grated orange peel (or tangerine, grapefruit, kumquat, etc.)
dash of lemon juice (optional)
½ cup seedless raisins
6 cups all-purpose flour (unbleached, soya, white flours)
yolk of an egg mixed with water

Topping:
Combine
¼ cup brown sugar (preferably light)
2 tablespoons grated citrus fruit
2 tablespoons chopped pecans (or your favorite nuts)

Dissolve yeast in water in the large mixing bowl. Stir in salt, sugar, butter, egg, egg white, citrus peel, and half the flour. Beat for 3 minutes, first at low speed, then at medium speed for 3 more minutes (with spoon a vigorous 300 strokes). Scrape sides of bowl and stir in raisins (wooden spoon, please), slowly beat in rest of flour until fully blended.

Cover with a clean cloth (or waxed paper and towel), and let rise in a warm place for nearly an hour, until bubbly-doubled. Stir down and beat for 30 seconds.

Spoon into a greased casserole, brush egg-yolk–water mixture over surface, and sprinkle topping mixture over all, pressing lightly with fingers. Bake in a 375° F. oven for nearly an hour, or until autumn brown. Cool on rack. (Won't get cool, 'tis said.)

"A good example is the best sermon."—FULLER

Dad's Homemade Raisin Bread

Traditionally, Wednesday was Raisin Bread Day at our home and bakery. Customers came from far and wide for the spicy-rich breads and rolls.

2 packages active dry yeast
¼ cup warm water
1½ teaspoons salt
¼ cup brown sugar
¼ cup butter (margarine)
1 cup milk, scalded
1 well-beaten egg

1 egg white, beaten
2 teaspoons cinnamon
½ teaspoon nutmeg
2 cups seedless raisins
6 cups sifted all-purpose flour
melted shortening
1 tablespoon granulated sugar

Dissolve yeast in water in large bowl, and let stand while you combine milk, brown sugar, butter, and salt in another bowl and cool to lukewarm. Stir into yeast mixture; add the egg and dry ingredients, stirring the while. Mix until well blended and smooth.

Turn out onto lightly floured board; knead until elastically smooth. Place in greased bowl, cover with clean cloth, let rise in warm place until doubled in bulk (nearly 2 hours). Punch down; turn out on lightly floured board. Again knead a few times for the luck of the Irish, and mold into one large loaf and place in greased loaf pan.

Brush top with melted shortening, and cover with clean cloth; let rise until double in bulk. Brush top with egg white, sprinkle with granulated sugar, and bake in 350° F. oven for nearly 45 minutes.

VARIATION. Instead of a loaf, after last kneading cut into thirds. Form each into a foot-long roll, place on greased cookie sheet; braid; pinch and seal ends. Then continue as above, but try confectioners' topping (See page 157) for sparkling goodness.

"Be slow in choosing a friend, slower in changing."
—BENJAMIN FRANKLIN

My Uncle John's Favorite Raisin Bread

Deliciously rich and sweet toasted or plain. Another Wednesday special.

1 package active dry yeast
½ cup warm water
½ cup milk or buttermilk, scalded
1½ teaspoons salt
¼ cup sugar
¼ cup soft butter or margarine

1 cup seedless raisins, light or dark
2 eggs, beaten
4 cups all-purpose flour
2 cups water, blended with
1 cup confectioners' sugar

Dissolve yeast in the warm water. Combine milk, sugar, salt, butter, raisins; stir until sugar is completely dissolved. Cool to lukewarm; stir in half the flour; beat well until doughy-soft. Add eggs and slowly add more flour, until dough is fairly soft, beating well. Turn out on a lightly floured board or table, knead till dough is elastically smooth, adding flour if needed.

Place in greased bowl, turn over once, cover with clean cloth, and let rise for nearly 2 hours in a warm place. Punch down, turn out on a lightly floured surface, cut in half, shape into loaves (or balls for greased pan or earthenware), place in greased bread pans. Cover again, and let rise for an hour. Then bake in a 350° F. oven for 45 minutes (or 375° F. oven for 30 minutes).

Remove from pans to cooling racks. Combine 1 cup confectioners' sugar and enough water (milk) to make a good running topping. Spread on tops of loaves with knife, or spoon it on lengthwise or widthwise. (You will be more than pleased with the appearance, and taste.)

"On the plains of hesitation bleach the bones of countless millions who at the dawn of victory sat down to rest and, resting, died."—GEORGE W. CECIL

Dad's Raisin-Oatmeal Batter Bread

This was a real healthful favorite on Raisin Bread Day.

1 package active dry yeast	2 tablespoons soft shortening
2 cups warm water	4 cups sifted all-purpose flour
1½ teaspoons salt	1 cup rolled oats
3 tablespoons sugar	½ cup seedless raisins

Dissolve yeast in water in large mixing bowl. Stir in salt, sugar, and shortening, plus 1 cup flour and rolled oats, stirring, stirring. Beat for 3 minutes (about 300 good hand strokes); then stir in rest of flour and raisins, mixing until smooth and satiny.

Cover with a clean cloth, and let rise in warm place until doubled. Stir down and continue for a count of 15 (slowly, now). Spoon into a greased loaf pan. Cover with a clean cloth, and let rise to that thumb-knuckle distance from top of pan and bake in a 360° F. oven for 50 minutes.

Remove to rack, brush with shortening or your favorite topping.

"To choose time is to save time."—BACON

SOY-FLOUR BREADS

The story of the soybean rivals wheat in excitement and historical significance for nations and peoples. It is one of the world's great protein foods, containing more than 2½ times as much protein as meat itself—plus vitamins, thiamine, niacin, riboflavin, calcium, phosphorus, and iron! The soybean is so interesting that its story could grip you as it did me before World War II, and you will want to find out all about the little bean!

Much of the oil has been freed from the soybean flour; hence it is very palatable and nutritional. It is truly a food of real merit. As the flour man stated to Dad: "The Soviets classify it as 'our little Chinese ally.'" (A bit dated!)

I don't believe one could overemphasize the value of soybean flour in the diets of the youth of our great country. Here is a vital food wrapped up in its own nutritional cloak.

My enthusiastic, hard-working father had done a vast amount of research on the attributes of soybean flour, experimenting and baking, and packaging a quick-mix flour long before the modern easy mixes, but when a young diabetic of a fine Council Bluffs family appeared on the scene, told by physicians to find a good loaf of soybean bread, Dad really went into the soybean-bread business. His bread and mixes were shipped and carried all over the country!

The following mixes are tried and true, used over and over until the morning of his death before Christmas in 1940, and still used to this day in homes and bakeries.

"We must be as courteous to a man as we are to a picture, to which we are willing to give the advantage of a good light."
—RALPH WALDO EMERSON

Dad's Soybean Yeast Bread

1 cake of compressed yeast   2 teaspoons salt
   (or starter)   1½ tablespoons shortening
2 tablespoons sugar   5 cups flour (all-purpose)
1 cup skim milk, scalded   1 cup soybean flour

Dissolve yeast and sugar in lukewarm milk (after scalding) in large bowl; let stand for 30 minutes. Stir in shortening, salt, and flour; mix until smooth. Turn out on lightly floured board, and knead for about 10 minutes. Cover with a clean cloth and let rise in a warm place for 30 minutes. Knead again for about 60 seconds. Please repeat this rising and kneading two more times. (Soybean flour demands this attention.)

Mold into loaf, place into greased loaf pan, cover, and let rise for about an hour; the dough will rise above the pan. Bake in a 375° F. oven for nearly 1 hour.

VARIATION. Whole-wheat–soybean bread with this healthful recipe consists of 1 cup soybean flour, 2 cups whole-wheat flour, 3 cups white flour (plus all other ingredients).

Dad's Famous Diabetic Bread

Father's last recipe for the trade—the climax of his good life with Mother.

2 tablespoons dry yeast   ¾ cup soybean flour
1¼ tablespoons salt   3 cups warm water
6 cups gluten flour

Dissolve yeast and salt in water in large bowl. Add soybean flour, stirring slowly; add the gluten flour and mix well into a soft dough. Cover with a clean cloth, let rise until almost doubled in bulk, then punch dough down, and let rise 30 minutes more.

Turn out onto a lightly floured board; cut into loaf sizes. (A scale is a mighty handy tool in bread-baking.) Mold into balls, shape into loaves, place into greased loaf pans. Let rise for 30 minutes. Then bake in a 350° F. oven for about 50 minutes.

Braué's All-American Soybean-Wheat Bread

Dad's specialty for all regular diets.

1 cake compressed yeast
2 tablespoons sugar
1 cup skim milk, scalded
1½ tablespoons shortening
1¾ teaspoons salt

4 cups soft-wheat flour
¼ cup soybean flour (or ⅛ cup soybean)
1⅛ cup whole-wheat, and
1¾ cup white flour

Dissolve yeast and sugar in milk in large bowl; let stand for 30 minutes. Add salt, shortening, and flour; blend well, mixing until smooth. Turn out on lightly floured board. Knead for about 10 minutes. Cover with a clean cloth, and let rise in a warm place for 30 minutes. Knead again for 30 seconds. Repeat the rising and kneading twice.

Shape into a loaf, place into a greased loaf pan, and let rise until doubled in size. Bake in a 370° F. oven for 1 hour. These make superior buns, or Parker House rolls too (at 380° F. for 20 minutes).

Dad's Healthful Soy–Whole-Wheat Bread

Soy flour combined with whole-grain flour is very successful, since it does not contain gluten itself. Soy-flour bread browns readily, so reduce the oven heat by 25° F. when substituting soy flour for any grain flours.

2 packages active dry yeast
3 cups milk, scalded, cooling to warm
1 tablespoon honey (molasses, syrup, or your choice)
2 tablespoons molasses (optional or any of the other sorghums that you wish)
a bit over 1 teaspoon salt, blended with
½ cup nutritional brewers' yeast (optional)
6 cups whole-wheat flour
2 cups soy flour

Dissolve the yeast in 1 cup of milk and the honey. Set aside while you blend dry ingredients. Mix all the other ingredients with half the blended dry ingredients. Add to yeast mixture. After beating until smooth, stir in remaining flour mixture.

Cover and place in a warm spot and let rise for 2 hours. Turn out on a lightly floured board and knead for 6 minutes. Divide equally and shape into loaves. Place in greased bread pans or oiled casserole dishes. Cover, and let rise in a warm place for at least 30 minutes.

Bake in a 350° F. oven for 50 minutes.

"Advice is least heeded when most needed."—English saying

Braué Soybean Farmers' Favorite

An all-time hit with persons who do not have to watch their diets, but excellent for individuals of sedentary habits too.

2 tablespoons dry yeast	⅓ cup bran
2 cups water (110° F.)	¼ cup milk, scalded (skim or
1½ tablespoons salt	nonfat dry)
2½ tablespoons sugar	2½ tablespoons corn meal
⅓ cup oatmeal	3 tablespoons soybean flour
¼ cup shortening	5 cups all-purpose flour

Dissolve yeast in water in large bowl; add milk and blend all the other ingredients, mixing well until firm and smooth. Cover with a clean cloth, let rise in a warm place for 45 minutes.

Turn out on a lightly floured board, knead gently for 10 minutes. Mold into balls, shape into loaves, and place into greased pans. Cover and let rise until dough is a bit above edge of pan.

Bake in 350° F. oven for nearly 1 hour.

"Modesty is the only sure bait when you angle for praise."
—CHESTERFIELD

Variation of Dad's Diabetic Bread

I still received orders for this healthful loaf while in the Army during World War II.

¼ cup dry yeast
½ cup warm water
¾ tablespoon salt
¾ tablespoon shortening
6 cups gluten flour

2 cups of warm water (110° F.)
1 cup soybean flour
⅔ cup evaporated milk

Dissolve yeast in ½ cup warm water in large bowl. Add salt, shortening, dry ingredients, and liquids, and mix with electric mixer for 40 minutes. (Gluten needs to be developed by mixing, but please do not overmix, as gluten will break down in the dough.)

Mold and shape into loaves, place in greased loaf pans, cover with a clean cloth, and let rise for 30 minutes. Bake in 350° F. oven for nearly an hour.

Soybean flour should be blended with other flours first, for better performance. Soybean flour absorbs much more water than wheat flours, so please be on guard—the dough is quite stiff, too.

HINT. Gluten bread requires more yeast than white bread. Mold and shape soybean-gluten dough into loaves soon after proofing (rising).

"Do not hang all on one nail."—German saying

Dad's Soybean-Oatmeal Bread

One of the most distinctly different and flavorful loaves ever, anywhere!

2 packages quick dry yeast
1 cup warm water
½ cup brown sugar
2 cups quick oats (or uncooked regular)
2½ cups boiling water

3 tablespoons shortening
4 teaspoons salt
6 cups all-purpose white flour
2 tablespoons wheat germ
1 cup nonfat dry milk
1 cup stirred soybean flour

Dissolve yeast in warm water in small bowl; then add brown sugar and stir a bit. Let stand for a few moments. Now in a large bowl mix together oats, boiling water, shortening, and salt; cool to lukewarm while blending together white flour, wheat germ, dry milk, and soybean flour in another bowl. Stir the yeast mixture into the oatmeal mixture, stirring, stirring while you slowly add the dry ingredients. Beat until satiny-smooth.

Turn out on a lightly floured board; knead well! Place in a large greased bowl, brush lightly with oil or shortening, cover with a clean cloth, and let rise until doubled in bulk (30 minutes). Punch down dough, fold edges over, turn upside down in bowl, cover, let rise 15 minutes.

Turn onto lightly floured board, cut into portions, and shape into loaves, placing them in greased loaf pans. Brush lightly with oil or melted shortening, cover, and let rise in a warm place until loaves are almost doubled in bulk (30 minutes). Bake in a 345° F. oven for nearly an hour.

HINT. Soybean flour calls for reduced amount of shortening in recipes, as it contains approximately 20 per cent fat and 2 per cent lecithin.

"Whatever advice you give, be short."—HORACE

SALT-RISING AND OTHER BREADS

Rahn Salt-Rising Bread

Salt-rising bread is leavened by the fermentation of flour and milk. Bacteria are most important actors in this play. The yeast plants of the air find the batter a good stage for development. Salt-rising bread needs more heat while fermenting and a much longer time to bake. Here is a good example.

2 tablespoons corn meal	1 quart milk
½ pint water	1 teaspoon salt
½ teaspoon salt	8 cups flour (variable)

Stir 2 tablespoons of corn meal into ½ pint of water heated to 130° F. Add ½ teaspoon of salt and mix very well. Put this in a jar or crock, cover, and place it in a pan of water at 160° F. Keep overnight in a warm place.

In the morning, warm 1 quart of milk; add 1 teaspoon salt and enough warm flour to make a heavy batter. Gradually dd the overnight corn meal and beat well for a few moments. Cover and keep in a warm place about 2 hours.

Gradually add flour and beat mix until it becomes a very soft dough. Turn out on a floured board and knead until it is elastically smooth. Divide equally into 4 portions, mold into loaves, and place each in a greased bread pan. Cover with a clean cloth and keep in a warm place for ½ hour.

Bake in a 350° F. oven for 1 hour.

"Heaven would be often unjust if it answered all our prayers."

Dad's Old-fashioned Salt-Rising Bread

Many adherents to this old-fashioned prize.

Into a bowl containing 4 cups of starter (sour or farmer's), add 1 teaspoon of salt, 1 teaspoon of soda, and 4 cups all-purpose flour (or a blend). Stir this sponge well and set aside to let rise.

Stir into starter sponge 1 cup milk (scalded and cooled to lukewarm), 2 tablespoons butter, 1 teaspoon sugar, and 6 cups of flour (variable). Turn out to lightly floured board, knead a bit, mold into loaves. Place in greased pans. Cover, and let rise for a spell. Bake in 350° F. oven for nearly an hour.

Aunt Chick of pie-baking fame allows that the rays of ole Sol for dough rising will make bread that much better!

"The whole of virtue consists in its practice."—CICERO

Cousin Gerta's Salt-Rising Bread

First Sponge:

1 cup milk, scalded	1 teaspoon salt
2 tablespoons corn meal	2 teaspoons sugar

Mix all ingredients and let rise overnight. In the morning mix the second sponge and add to the first.

Second Sponge:

1 cup water, lukewarm	1 tablespoon sugar
1 teaspoon salt	2 tablespoons shortening
	2 cups flour

Thoroughly incoporate with the first sponge, cover, and let rise until light. Then add—

3 cups flour

Mix until "smoothingly stiff." Turn out onto lightly floured table, knead well, mold into loaves, and place into greased pans. Brush tops of loaves with shortening. Cover and let rise for a spell. Bake in a 375° F. oven for 10 minutes, then at 350° F. for 30 minutes.

Mother's Friend Sophie's Salt-Rising Bread

Sophie's dramatic conversation, her bread, and spicy tea were just as exciting as the ride over to her house in the surrey.

1 tablespoon corn meal
1 teaspoon sugar
a bit of baking soda and
a pinch of ginger
¼ cup milk, scalded
a bit of salt

a handful of flour
½ cup boiling water (or potato water)
½ cup cold milk
4 cups flour

Blend corn meal, sugar, soda, and ginger. Add milk and stir slowly and well. Cover lightly and let mixture rest at room temperature overnight.

In the fairly early morning add a bit of salt and a handful of flour. Stir and let it rest for an hour. Then add boiling water, cold milk, and flour. Stir well; sprinkle with flour. Cover and let rest for an hour.

Turn out onto a lightly sprinkled board, cut dough equally, mold into loaves, and place in greased bread pans. Cover and let rise until doubled in bulk.

Bake in a 375° F. oven for 10 minutes. Lower heat to 350° F. and continue baking for 30 minutes more.

"Remember downtown Wanamaker's at Christ Tide?—sedate and gracious with the towering Christmas tree near the yawning stairs emitting the memorable organ music?"

Dad's Soldier-Days Ash Bread

On der hike mit der troops.

1 teaspoon salt
1 tablespoon soda
1 cup buttermilk

1 tablespoon fat
2 cups corn meal
water to make thick dough

Mix all well. Pull out the ashes of a good hot hearth fire (or campfire) and make a nest in them for the dough. Place dough in nest. Let it rest awhile until it forms a crust. Then cover with ashes and hot embers and bake for 30 minutes.

Uncle Chris' Indian Chestnut Bread

A life-saver along the olden trail . . . now, good for campouts.

1 pound chestnuts, peeled and scaled (of inside skin)
enough cornmeal and boiling water for a mix

Mix well. Wrap in green corn shucks (or, to be modern, foil), tying securely with twine. Boil in water for 2 hours.

INDIAN BEAN BREAD. This is prepared the same way. Just add ½ teaspoon soda to the mix. This mix may also be boiled, uncovered, in ball form in less time.

"Do you remember in the days 'that were never long enough' that the potato in the spout of the kerosene can was a must?"

CRACKERS, ZWIEBACK AND BREAD STICKS

Crackers

Crackers may be baked from most bread batches. For example, reserve some of the bread dough, work in a touch bit of flour, roll dough out and cut into desired geometric design. Prick tops with fork (to let out bubbles) and bake on greased sheet for 10 to 12 minutes in 325°–350° F. oven.

"Let us be of good cheer, remembering that the misfortunes hardest to bear are those which never come."—J. R. LOWELL

Zwieback

Roll bread dough, after last rising, into small balls. Place them on greased baking sheet; rest them a bit, and bake them in a 350° F. oven for 12 minutes. Let cool, then cut them in halves with sharp knife. Return them to a 200° F. oven for complete baking until crispy-brown.

"The winds and waves are always on the side of the able navigators."—EDWARD GIBBON

Rolls

Shape dough into desired shapes, place on greased baking sheet, let rest for short rising period. Bake in 375°–400° F. oven for 12 to 15 minutes. Reduce shortening by at least 1 tablespoon if egg is used for flavoring. Raisins and cinnamon provide two of the many variations.

Bread Sticks

Roll out dough to ¼–½-inch thickness, cut strips of 2 by 6 to 9 inches. Roll into sticks, place on greased baking tins, and brush with cold water (or egg wash). Sprinkle with coarse salts (salt, onion, garlic, etc.) and seeds (caraway, dill, sesame, etc.), and bake in a 400° F. oven for 15 minutes.

"An education isn't how much you have committed to memory, or even how much you know. It's being able to differentiate between what you do know and what you don't. It's knowing where to go to find out what you need to know; and it's knowing how to use the information once you get it."—WILLIAM FEATHER

Other Memories From
The Bakery Kitchen

"Give what you have to someone; it may be better than you dare to think."—HENRY WADSWORTH LONGFELLOW

"The only thing necessary for evil to triumph is for good men to do nothing."—EDMUND BURKE

"Challenging, difficult work is a privilege and the wasting of time and talent a cardinal sin."
　　　　　　　　　　—ANNE L. BOWES of her mother, KATE

THE BAKING OF HAMS AND POULTRY

One of the many pleasant memories of my parents and the bakeshop stems from countless requests from churches, clubs, and neighbors for the Braué meat-baking procedure.

This process was accomplished at the end of the baking day, when the large oven was cooling. Throughout the years Dad wrapped thousands of hams, hens, geese, and turkeys in pumpernickel or dark-flour doughs and baked them in shallow pans, utilizing the lessening heat of the oven for full and even baking. This method was a forerunner of the aluminum-wrapped process of modern baking or barbecuing, as were fish baked in corn shucks, and mud-wrapped Murphies!

Dad made sure the dough was joined at the top so that the natural juices steeped within the dough wrapping. Ladies, try this magnificent baking method in your oven or barbecue, as follows.

HAMS. Bake the whole ham fat side up in a 300°–325° F. oven, 25 minutes per pound for tenderized hams, 30 minutes per pound for nontenderized.

POULTRY AND GAME. In a 325° F. oven bake small birds, up to 5 pounds, 30 minutes per pound. For birds weighing more than 5 pounds, and for game, bake 25 minutes per pound.

Basic Bread Stuffing
Enough for the family bird!

5 quarts bread crumbs (preferably a few days old)
2¼ teaspoons salt
¼ teaspoon pepper
1½ teaspoons poultry seasoning, or celery salt
¾ cup minced onions
¼ cup diced celery
1¼ cups butter or salad oil

Use one cup of stuffing for each pound of bird.

Holiday Bread Stuffing

For a most flavorful bread stuffing for the holiday bird, place 4 slices of bread (white or dark) in cold water in a mixing bowl and squeeze out until spongy. Drizzle with melted butter. While this is soaking, blend 1 teaspoon salt, ¼ teaspoon poultry seasoning, ⅛ teaspoon black pepper, 1 teaspoon chopped parsley, and 1 teaspoon grated onion with 1 beaten egg. Add egg mixture to bread mixture with some chopped cooked giblets—and you have a bread stuffing that should please all branches of the family!

"Remember when an attic was a rainy-day refuge, a room wonders—not a do-it-yourself extra room?"

HOME-RENDERED LARD

For the finest of pastries, cakes and breads!

This method was used for years by our bakery's good neighbor, Pace's Meat Market, a complete butchery and packing plant. The author bouncingly remembers riding Pace's two-wheeled delivery pony cart, pridefully running errands while hanging on for dear life!

Remove the back fat, leaf, and fat trimmings. Wash and chill. Cut into small chunks; then place pieces in a heavy kettle, but do not fill, and cook slowly at 210°–212° F., stirring to avoid sticking. The temperature will rise as water evaporates, but do not let it go higher than 250°–255° F. As water evaporates, brown cracklings will begin to float. (Reserve the cracklings for quick-bread batters.) They sink to the bottom when the lard is nearly rendered. Do not let them stick to the bottom and scorch.

Complete rendering makes better lard, as most of the water is removed, preventing water-souring during storage of lard. Chill immediately, covering tightly in freezer container, refrigerator, or other cool place. Mix a little shortening with lard for flavoring; antioxidants can be purchased at ice plants, packing houses, and locker-storage plants.

"When time flies it cannot be recalled."—VIRGIL

AUF WIEDERSEHEN!

It has been an honor and prideful pleasure to have been able to share just a few of the thousands of family "bread winners" with you all. There are more books in der oldt mill . . .

We hope to be able to publish revised editions of *Uncle John's Original Bread Book* at frequent intervals. In the meantime, your questions about Rahn-Braué bread recipes (and about the Uncle John's Original Home Bakery franchise) will be answered by addressing

> UNCLE JOHN
> P. O. Box 3276
> Midland, Texas 79704

J. R. B.

"Eat your sunshine in bread!"

INDEX

"Whatever begins also ends."—SENECA